Sketch of Kingston Market Place by Thomas Rowlandson, *c.*1800

G000090635

KINGSTON
UPON
THAMES
A Pictorial History

Queen's Promenade and the river, *c*.1900.

KINGSTON UPON THAMES

A Pictorial History

Anne McCormack

Phillimore

1989

Published by
PHILLIMORE & CO. LTD.
Shopwyke Hall, Chichester, Sussex

© The Mayor and Burgesses of
The Royal Borough of Kingston upon Thames, 1989

ISBN 0 85033 716 X

Printed and bound in Great Britain by
BIDDLES LTD.
Guildford, Surrey

List of Illustrations

Frontispiece: Queen's Promenade and the river, *c*.1900

Foreword and Acknowledgements

In writing this book I am aware that a number of publications have already appeared which depict Kingston's past in pictures. Of these Bryan Woodriff's *Kingston Upon Thames as it was* (1980), Colin Cornish's *Royal Kingston's Heritage* (1987), and Kingston Heritage Centre's portfolios of street scenes, theatres and inns in Kingston and district, are the most comprehensive. In the present book I have selected pictures depicting aspects of life in Kingston, Surbiton and Malden and Coombe, mainly of the 19th and early 20th centuries. I have attempted to find sources which have not been used extensively before but, if some duplicates from past publications have crept in, it is because they are of sufficient merit to justify their republication or because they illustrate a point or tell an interesting story.

I am most grateful for the help I have received from my colleagues in Kingston Heritage Centre, including Miss M. Shipley, Heritage Officer, Mrs. A. Baker, Antiquities Officer, Mr. C. Cornish, Local History Officer and Mr. R. O'Connell and Mr. S. Davies, Kingston Heritage Oral History Team. I should also like to thank Dr. D. B. Robinson, County Archivist, and my colleagues in Surrey Record Office; Mr. R. L. Barrett-Cross, A.M.R.S.H., Historian, Royal Army Medical Corps; Mr. D. Coomber, Surbiton Lawn Tennis and Squash Rackets Club; Mrs. A. Lansdell, Curator, Weybridge Museum; Mr. B. Morrissey, British Aerospace; Miss J. Sampson, Features Editor, *Surrey Comet*; and Mr. J. Woodroffe, former Curator, Regimental Museum, Clandon Park, for their patience and valuable advice, and also Mr. L. Kirkin, Mr. K. Simmons and Mr. H. Lansdell for photography. I also wish to acknowledge the late Miss J. Wakeford, whose research papers have been invaluable, and I thank all those listed below who have allowed their pictures to be reproduced in this book. I apologise if any copyright ownership exists of which I am not aware or which I have been unable to trace.

Sources for Illustrations

Kingston Borough Archives: 1, 13, 14 (courtesy of Mr. B. Woodriff), 18a & b, 21a & b, 32, 43a-d, 55 (courtesy of Rosemary Wren), 74a & b (courtesy of Mr. B. Woodriff), 102, 106, 116, 121, 122 (courtesy of Mr. J. Murton), 123, 124, 125 (courtesy of Miss D. Compton), 126b, 127, 128a & b, 129 (courtesy of the *Surrey Comet*), 130, 134, 146, 148.

Kingston Heritage Oral History Record: 67 (courtesy of Mr. M. Reilly), 69a & b (courtesy of Mrs. M. Surman), 71a & b (courtesy of Miss P. Wild), 78a & b (courtesy of Mrs. Eagles), 81a, 82a & b (courtesy of Mr. P. Parslow), 118b.

Kingston Heritage Centre: Local History Collection, front endpaper, 2-9, 11-12, 16a, 17, 18c, 19-20, 23-28, 30-31, 35, 37-38, 40-42, 45-53, 56, 58-59, 60-63, 66, 68, 70, 72-73, 76-77, 79-80, 83-86, 95-97, 99-100, 103-104, 107, 109-111, 114b, 115, 118a, 119-120, 132-133, 138-144, 145a & b, 147, 149-154.

Surrey Record Office: 10 (*Illustrated London News*), 22, 29, 39, 54 (courtesy of the Headmaster, Kingston Grammar School), 57 (courtesy of the Principal, Hillcroft College), 88, 98a & b, 101 (courtesy of the Vicar, St Paul's, Hook), 105, 112, 113, 126a (courtesy of the Vicar, St Mark's, Surbiton), 131, 156 (courtesy of the Headmaster, Kingston Grammar School).

Guildford Muniment Room: 16b (courtesy of Dennis Specialist Vehicles). *Beaulieu Motor Museum*: 34. *Bodleian Library*: 155 (John Johnson Collection: Bicycles, 3). *British Aerospace*: 33, 65a & b, 157. *British Library*: back endpaper. *Mr. P. Gerhold and Mr. L. Bowerman*: 137. *Mrs. D. Judge*: 36. *Kingston Wel-Care Association*: 108. *Regimental Museum, Clandon Park*: 15, 87. *The Vicar, St John the Baptist, Kingston Vale*: 89-92. *Surrey Comet*: 44, 75, 81b, 114a (courtesy of Miss J. Sampson), 117. *Mr. M. Turk*: 64. *The Minister, Kingston United Reformed church*: 93, 94, 136. *Wimbledon Lawn Tennis Museum*: 135.

Celebrating Kingston's Past

The present Royal Borough of Kingston upon Thames lies to the south-west of London. It comprises the three former boroughs of Kingston, Malden and Coombe, and Surbiton which were united to form one of 32 London boroughs under the London Government Act of 1963.

The early civic history of the ancient Royal Borough of Kingston is well known (*see*, for example, June Sampson, *The Story of Kingston*, 1972; June Sampson, *All Change: Kingston, Surbiton and New Malden in the 19th century*, 1985; and Royal Borough of Kingston upon Thames, *Royal Kingston*, 1988).

In 838 an important ecclesiastical council was held in the town and the record of its proceedings in the British Library provides the first written reference to Kingston by name. The town can also claim the distinction of being the crowning place of seven Anglo-Saxon kings in the tenth century: Edward the Elder, Athelstan, Edmund, Edred, Edwy, Edward the Martyr and Ethelred. The large stone preserved outside the present Guildhall, now a scheduled ancient monument, has been revered by generations of Kingstonians as the ceremonial coronation stone on which kings were crowned more than one thousand years ago.

Formerly in the county of Surrey, the town was an important royal manor by the time of the Domesday Survey of 1086. It then boasted a church, five mills and three salmon fisheries from which the Borough derives the three fishes on its coat of arms.

By a succession of royal charters – 34 in all granted between 1200 and 1964 – the town gradually gained administrative independence from the county of Surrey. Official borough status was achieved in 1481 by a Charter of Incorporation granted by Edward IV.

The position of Kingston at an easily fordable place near the Thames ensured its early success as a market and trading centre, encouraged in the 16th century by the proximity of Hampton Court. A bridge has played a crucial part in Kingston's history from at least the 12th century.

In spite of the loss of many historic buildings, the inevitable changes caused by modern developments and the traffic needs of the 20th century, the people of Kingston have always celebrated the anniversaries of important historical events with enthusiasm, as the following illustrations bear witness.

1. Aerial view of central Kingston, 1935. This photograph, taken just after the construction of the present Guildhall, is a reminder of how the centre of Kingston has altered over the last half-century. Behind the Guildhall a row of shops along St James' Road has been replaced by the County Court (1959) and the first Guildhall extension (1976). The land beside the Guildhall (to the left of the picture) is now the site of a second Guildhall extension (1981) and a Police Station (1969). Opposite, on the river side of the High Street, is the Odeon Cinema, demolished in 1988, and along the river towards the Market Place is the site scheduled (1989) for the Charter Quay development. Courage's, formerly Hodgson's brewery (bottom right), was replaced in 1973 by a large complex of shops and offices. To the north-east of the bridge and just visible in the picture is the Horse Fair site, now covered by the John Lewis development (under construction 1988/89).

2. Certified copy made in 1912 of the arms and seals of the Royal Borough recorded by the Heralds in 1623. The three salmon on the arms and the corporate seal (bottom left) are a reminder of Kingston's three famous Domesday fisheries. The Court of Record seal (bottom right) depicts the letter 'K' and a barrel or tun which is a pun on the town's name. The arms were first recorded by the Heralds in 1572. The two seals were in use from at least the 15th century.

England became a Kingdom, Anno Domini 819.
England in 1850 is ruled by a Descendant of her first King.

Kingston-on-Thames.
THE INAUGURATION
OF THE
CORONATION STONE
OF THE
ANGLO SAXON KINGS,
THE ANCESTORS OF OUR
ILLUSTRIOUS QUEEN,
WILL TAKE PLACE ON
THURSDAY, the 19th of SEPTEMBER,
WITH MASONIC HONOURS.

AT ONE O'CLOCK,

The Right Worshipful the PROVINCIAL GRAND MASTER of the FREEMASONS of Surrey attended by the Brethren of the Province and other Masons, will meet his WORSHIP THE MAYOR, attended by the Corporation and Burgesses and Visitors at the TOWN HALL, and go in procession to the MONUMENT.

AT TWO O'CLOCK,

A Public Dejeuner for LADIES AND GENTLEMEN will be provided in the Grounds of CHARLES ROWLLS, ESQ., kindly granted for the occasion.

AT HALF-PAST FOUR O'CLOCK,

The CHILDREN of the SCHOOLS will sing the NATIONAL ANTHEM, and be presented at the Monument with Books and Medals.

AT HALF-PAST FIVE,

A series of AQUATIC SPORTS will take place at Town's-End.

AT SEVEN O'CLOCK,

A GRAND DISPLAY of FIREWORKS on the Thames
By Southby, WILL CONCLUDE THE FESTIVITIES OF THE DAY.
MILITARY BANDS WILL ATTEND.

TICKETS for the Dejeuner at 7s. 6d. each, including Wine and a Medal may be obtained on or before Monday, the 16th instant, of Messrs. Shrubsole, Ranyard, Gould, Hollingdale, E. Phillips, and Henry H. Young, Esq., Town's-End, Kingston; Mr. Furze, Greyhound Hotel, Richmond; Mr. Henry Lamb, Chertsey; Messrs. Russell, Guildford; Mr. J. White, Dorking; Mr. Wigzell, Epsom; G. Morrison, Esq., Reigate; and in London of Mr. Taylor, Medalist, 33, Little Queen Street; Mr. S. Sainsbury, 177, Strand; Messrs. Eastman and Yeo, 100, Cheapside; and Messrs. Barclay & Son, 170, Regent Street.

The beautiful Medal by Taylor, and the Genealogical Chart of the Queen's descent from the Anglo Saxon Kings will be ready for Sale on the day of inauguration.

H. I. FRICKER, PRINTER, MARKET-PLACE, KINGSTON.

459

PRESENTED BY COUNCILLOR F. J. GOODMAN
31st JANUARY. 1924.

3a. & b.   Poster for the inauguration of the Coronation Stone in 1850 (*opposite*) and a view of the Stone in its former position, *c*.1895-1904 (*above*). The Coronation Stone, which had previously been used as a mounting block for horsemen, was surrounded by ornamental railings and formally inaugurated as a monument on 19 September 1850. It was placed in front of Clattern House which stood on the present Guildhall site. Alderman Gould, who had been instrumental in organising the event, described it 50 years later in the *Surrey Comet*: 'the day of unveiling was kept as a public holiday. There were excursions from all parts of England to witness the ceremony and thousands of people came into the town. There was first a procession round the town. A medal was struck in honour of the occasion. Then there was a public breakfast in a large marquee.' (This was in the grounds of Kingston Hall, the home of John Rowlls, which stood next to his brewery in Brook Street.)

4. Celebrating the millennium of the crowning of Edward the Elder in Kingston in 1902. Edward was crowned in 901 but some of the events were celebrated in May 1902, the year of Edward VII's coronation, by a procession, sporting events and a balloon ascent. The procession, which wound its way through the streets of Kingston (seen here outside the Royal County Theatre in Fife Road), was over a mile long and just avoided heavy traffic going to the races at Hurst Park.

The Mayor received a telegram from the King wishing the town every success on the day. A tournament, maypole dancing and sporting events were held on the Dinton Road football field to which 'flocked a continuous stream of pleasure seekers, thousands of whom arrived at Kingston – 800 packed into one train and large numbers came by road from towns and villages in the locality' (*Surrey Comet*).

5. Moving the Coronation Stone in 1935. Clattern House, which had formerly housed the Council offices and public library, was demolished to make way for the present Guildhall. The Coronation Stone is seen here being moved prior to its re-erection alongside the new building. Whilst awaiting the preparation of a permanent site, the Stone had a temporary home in the Memorial Gardens in Union Street.

6. The crowning of King Athelstan enacted at the Three Towns' Pageant, 1951. King Athelstan was crowned King at Kingston in 925. The commemoration of the event in 1951 was organised by Kingston, Richmond and Twickenham at Hampton Court as part of the Festival of Britain celebrations. Queen Mary was one of the guests.

7a. & b. Celebrating the 700th anniversary of King John's Charter, 1899. A spectacular pageant made its way through the streets of Kingston on 26 April 1899 to celebrate the 700th anniversary of Kingston's first charter. By a miscalculation the event was held a year too early. The charter was granted in 1200. The day was observed by many as a holiday; schools closed and traders led the procession with their vehicles specially decorated for the occasion. Historical tableaux followed. In pride of place was King John performing, the *Surrey Comet* observed, 'one of the few good acts which marked his reign, the presentation of the charter to Kingston'.

8. Queen Elizabeth's visit to Kingston to commemorate the 400th anniversary of Kingston's Grammar School charter in 1561. Her Majesty is seen here leaving the Guildhall on her way to the school for a reception.

9. Excavation and preservation of a cellar from a medieval merchant's house, 1986. The cellar or 'undercroft' was originally discovered beneath the *Rose and Crown* public house on the Horse Fair in 1900. Its fate was subsequently unknown until its rediscovery, with its vaulted roof almost completely intact, by Museum of London archaeologists in 1985. The entire cellar was carefully excavated, encased and lifted by a gigantic crane in a massive operation in December 1986. Together with masonry work from Kingston's medieval bridge, it was temporarily stored in a Corporation Depot. In September 1988 the cellar and bridge remains were restored to the riverside ready for permanent display as historic monuments in the John Lewis Partnership development.

Civic Government and Public Services

The 19th century brought many changes in local government. For centuries Kingston had been governed by a self-perpetuating Council known as the Court of Assembly with two Bailiffs at its head, a High Steward (an honorary appointment), and a Learned Steward and a Recorder, who were members of the legal profession. Officers included a Town Clerk, appointed for life, and annually-elected Chamberlains (treasurers), Bridgewardens, Schoolwardens and Paving Wardens. They were assisted by minor officials responsible for the day-to-day running of the markets.

In 1773 an act for the 'better lighting and watching of the town and the preventment of nuisances' had placed in the hands of the Bailiffs, High Steward, Justices and others responsibility for the erection of glass lamps in public places, the appointment of up to 14 watchmen, and the prosecution of persons leaving 'ashes, dirt, dust, soil, straw, dung or any filth or annoyance' in the streets, paving the way for an increased awareness of safety and public health during the next century.

Under the Municipal Corporations Act of 1835 the Corporation was given the style of Mayor, Aldermen and Burgesses and elections became much freer. At the first meeting of the new Borough Council held on 1 January 1836 three committees for watching, finance and byelaws were established. In 1840 a fire brigade committee was appointed and a market committee in 1841. These tended to be *ad hoc* and it was not until 1855, under the Kingston upon Thames Improvement Act, that the 1773 Act was superseded and the committee structure formalised. This Act, a second Improvement Act in 1888, and several public acts ensured the appointment of separate committees to deal with public health, drainage, lighting, highways, education and building regulation. The Borough Council's powers were greatly extended in the 20th century to include many additional responsibilities, among them housing and planning. A borough police force was appointed in 1836 and in 1840 the Metropolitan Police assumed responsibility for the Borough.

Whilst Kingston was 'improving' itself, Surbiton and New Malden (both formerly part of Kingston Parish) began to develop as separate local authorities: Surbiton by its own Improvement Act in 1855 and New Malden in 1866 under the Public Health Act of 1848 and the Local Government Act of 1858. Surbiton Improvement Commission and New Malden Local Board both became, with extended boundaries, Urban Districts in 1894 and Borough Councils in 1936. Both boroughs of Surbiton and Malden and Coombe were amalgamated – or rather 're-united' – with Kingston in 1965 under the London Government Act of 1963. The new London Borough received a confirmation of its royal status in 1966.

10.   The opening of the Lambeth Water Company's Works at Seething Wells, 1852. John Aubrey, the historian, visited Kingston towards the end of the 17th century. To the south of the town he saw 'a spring that is cold in summer and warm in winter; it bubbles up and is called Seething Well. The inhabitants thereabouts do use to wash their eyes with it, and drink of it'. Near this site the Lambeth Water Company opened their works and a reservoir in 1852 and soon afterwards the Chelsea Water Company built theirs on adjoining land.

11.   The opening of Kingston's Sewage Works by the Mayor, Alderman East, on 6 November 1888. This was the culmination of over 25 years of struggle for a satisfactory system in the town. The works, constructed on part of Down Hall Meadow facing the Barge Walk, just below the railway bridge, were operated by the Native Guano Company. The ground floor of the main buildings housed the machinery whilst the upper storey was used for the sludge presses and for storing the bags of 'native guano' ready for sale. Advertisements in the local newspaper claimed it was the best and cheapest manure available for all kinds of crops.

12. Connecting with Surbiton sewage, *c*.1887-88. Agreement was reached in 1887 for Kingston to deal with Surbiton's sewage at its new works in Down Hall Meadow. This connecting main along the Portsmouth Road cost £7,000.

13. The opening of extensions to Malden and Coombe's Sewage Works in 1915. The original works, built on land near California Road, were complete and in operation by August 1888, three months before Kingston's were officially opened. The system was extended in 1895 to include Coombe and Old Malden and further work was undertaken between 1910 and 1915.

14. Aerial view of the site of the Native Guano Works (1888), the future site of the Electricity 'B' Station; the Gas Works (1854); and the old Electricity Power Station, later called the 'A' Station (1893). The barge and horse and cart seen in the foreground were used to transport coal to the power station.

15. King George VI's visit to Kingston on 27 October 1948 to open the Kingston 'B' Electricity Power Station on the site of the Native Guano Works. The station closed in 1980.

16a. & b.   The Kingston and Surbiton Fire Brigade at its station, 23 London Road, *c.*1900 (*above*), and Kingston's second motor appliance commissioned from Dennis Brothers of Guildford, in 1910 (*below*). A Kingston Borough Fire Brigade and Escape Brigade was formed in 1857 but was disbanded in 1881. Meanwhile a Kingston Volunteer Steam Brigade, which had been formed in 1870, was amalgamated in 1879 with the Surbiton District Brigade. Renamed the Kingston and Surbiton District Brigade, it operated six stations until, in 1919/20, the two sections parted company to be administered by Kingston Borough and Surbiton Urban District respectively. During the Second World War a national fire service was established but afterwards, in 1948, Surrey County Council assumed responsibility for the local fire service until the formation of the Greater London Council in 1965. The station in London Road was built in the 1880s and was occupied by the brigade until after the Second World War. New Malden had a separate fire service which was formed in 1886.

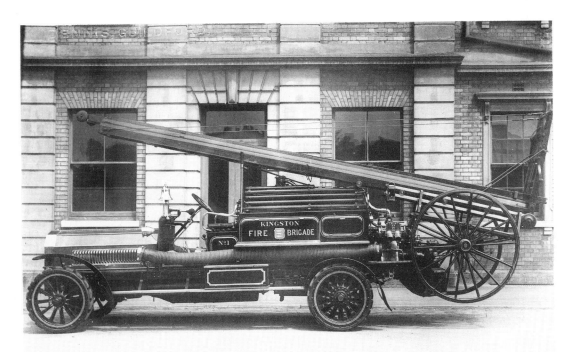

17.   The Malden section of the 'V' Division of the Metropolitan Police, 1910. The 'V' or Wandsworth Division of the Metropolitan Police was formed in 1830 and Kingston, Malden and Surbiton were brought within its jurisdiction in 1840. The Malden section is seen here outside the Police Station in Malden Road, now High Street.

18a. & b.   The present Guildhall, designed by Maurice Webb, was built in 1934/35 on the site of Clattern House, a fine mansion used in the early 19th century as a residence for the Assize Judges, and later as a public library and municipal offices. The new Guildhall was erected in record time, foundations to completion taking just nine months.

18c. Procession at the opening ceremony which was performed by Princess Alice, Duchess of Athlone (not in the picture), on 3 July 1935. The macebearer heading the procession was Thomas Parslow who retired in 1944 after 36 years in a position which had been held by his father and grandfather before him. The Mayor was Sir Alfred Woodgate. Others in the procession included Lady Ashcombe, wife of the Lord Lieutenant of Surrey; the Town Clerk, Mr. A. W. Forsdyke; the Recorder, Sir Thomas Inskip; the High Steward, the Earl of Middleton, and the High Sheriff of Surrey, Sir Laurence Halsey. The East Surrey Regiment were in attendance.

19.   The Mayor, Dr. W. E. St Lawrence Finny, conferring the Freedom of the
Borough on the Duke of Cambridge on 12 December 1898. The Duke
received the solid 15-carat gold key, symbolising his freedom, as a mark of
gratitude for his gift to the people of Kingston of the site for the Victoria
Hospital, which he had opened earlier in the day. The Duke is also pictured
(inset) placing a new Mayoress's chain, made from a design by Dr. Finny,
round the neck of the Mayoress.

20.   Field Marshal Sir Douglas Haig, Commander in Chief of the British Forces during the Great War
(who lived at Eastcott, Kingston Hill), at a reception given by the Mayor, C. H. Burge, following his
admission to the Freedom of the Borough in August 1919. A large crowd including many disabled,
demobilised men, who referred to the Field Marshal affectionately as 'Douggie', lined the procession route
and the Market Place. The Council Chamber was too small for the occasion so the ceremony was held,
instead, in the picturesque King's Hall of Nuthall's Restaurant in Thames Street. Tea was afterwards
served in Nuthall's riverside garden. The photograph was taken at the home of the Mayor in Crescent
Road.

21a. & b.   Sir Percy Vincent J.P., Lord Mayor of London, and the Lady Mayoress, in procession on 23 September 1936, the day Malden and Coombe became a Borough. The Charter of Incorporation was presented to the Charter Mayor, Major John E. Hill, O.B.E., by the Lord Mayor at Beverley Park. A Charter luncheon, displays of dancing, sporting events, community singing and a searchlight display by the 316th Anti-Aircraft Company, R.E., completed the celebrations. Children from local schools, numbering 3,500, attended the ceremony and were all provided with luncheon boxes and commemorative medals.

Road and Rail

At the beginning of the 19th century Kingston was a well known coaching town. According to Merryweather, the 19th-century local historian and politician, 'four and twenty coaches still ran through the market place' in the 1830s stopping at the *Sun* (later Woolworths), the *Coach and Horses* and the *Griffin*. Traffic on the old wooden bridge had become so congested that a new one made of stone was opened in 1828. Tolls were charged for another 42 years but finally, on 12 March 1870, amidst much local rejoicing, the bridge was declared toll-free by the Mayor.

The first railway station in the area was not in Kingston itself but at Surbiton which was for a time called Kingston-on-Railway. The London and Southampton Railway Company opened a small station on 21 May 1838 in a cutting not far from the present station. It was rebuilt in 1840 on the site it occupies today. The present building dates from 1938.

The railway came to Kingston proper when a station to the north of the town was opened on 1 July 1863. The *Surrey Comet* announced 'with great pleasure' the opening of the new line but added that the high fares charged for short distances had 'given rise to a great deal of grumbling ... no one would think of paying 9d. to Richmond when the omnibus serves to take them there for 6d.' An extension to Wimbledon via New Malden was opened on 1 January 1869. The line became known as the 'Kingston loop'.

The *Surrey Comet*'s comment on the cheapness of the omnibus fares foresaw the competition which would initially develop between rival services. Later in the 19th century, however, the coaches provided useful links between stations and attempted to synchronise their timetables with those of the railway companies. They also continued to serve isolated parts of the country throughout the century. Nostalgia, no doubt, also had a hand in their continuing popularity towards the end of the century.

Kingston Corporation initiated unsuccessful Tramway Bills in Parliament in 1871, 1882 and 1899 and rivalry caused friction between the Corporation and the London United Tramway Company. The latter was finally successful and the Mayor opened the system by driving a tram across Kingston bridge to 'hearty cheers' on 1 March 1906. The tramway system caused alterations to be made to many of Kingston's roads, including Clarence Street, and in 1914 the bridge was widened to cope with increased traffic. Upon the demise of the trams in 1931 trolley buses were introduced and their overhead lines became a feature of Kingston's streets until their removal in 1962.

The opening of Kingston By-Pass in October 1927, the first road of its kind in the country, acknowledged the demands of the commercial and private motor vehicle and, 60 years on, in 1986-89, the construction of a relief road to take through traffic away from the town-centre will enable many of the most popular shopping areas to be pedestrianised.

OPENING OF
KINGSTON BRIDGE,
FREE OF TOLL,
Saturday, March 12, 1870,
OFFICIAL PROGRAMME.

The Lord Mayor and the Sheriffs of Middlesex will be received on their arrival at the Station, by the Mayor, Corporation, Bridge Trustees, and other authorities, and a Guard of Honour of the 12th Royal Surrey Volunteers. The PROCESSION will then be formed in the following order:—

12th Surrey Rifle Volunteers.

Sir J. C. Lawrence, Chairman, Sir J. Thwaites and the other Members of the Joint Committee of the Corporation of London, and the Metropolitan Board of Works.

The City Chamberlain and Mr. Pollard.

The Bridge Trustees.

The Corporation and the Local Board Committee.

Band of the 3rd Royal Surrey Militia.

Captain Parratt and the Staff of the Regiment.

The Churchwardens of Kingston-on-Thames.

The Chairman of the East Molesey Local Board.

Chairman of the Surbiton Improvement Commission.

The Chairman of the Hampton Wick Local Board.

The Corporation of Kingston-upon-Thames.

The Under-Sheriff of Surrey.

The Under-Sheriffs of Middlesex.

The Borough Magistrates.

The County Magistrates.

The County Members.

THE MAYOR OF KINGSTON-UPON-THAMES.

The Lord High Steward.

The High Sheriff of Surrey.

The Sheriffs of Middlesex.

THE LORD MAYOR OF LONDON.

12th Surrey Rifle Volunteers.

As soon as the Lord Mayor's Carriage has passed over the Bridge, a Royal Salute of 21 guns will announce to the Town and neighbourhood that Kingston Bridge is once more TOLL FREE.

The Procession will start from the Station at 3.15 p.m. passing by Richmond Road, London Street, Eden Street, Market Place, Church Street, Clarence Street, over the Bridge to Hampton Wick, then by High Street, Park Road, St. John's Road, and Park Grove; returning by the Bridge, through Thames Street, to the Griffin Hotel, where a Déjeuner will be given to the Lord Mayor and other Officials.

In the Evening the Bridge will be Illuminated, and a Grand Display of Fireworks take place at the River Side.

G. PHILLIPSON, PRINTER, MARKET PLACE, KINGSTON.

22. A view of Kingston showing the old wooden bridge across the Thames in 1799. The bridge, dating from around 1200, was a flimsy wooden structure needing constant maintenance. Two Bridgewardens were appointed by the Corporation to supervise its administration. By the beginning of the 19th century its condition was so poor that Edward Lapidge, the County Surveyor, was commissioned to design a new one. This was opened by the Duchess of Clarence in 1828.

23. Programme announcing the opening of Kingston Bridge 'free of toll' in 1870. Tolls were charged for traffic coming over the wooden bridge during the 15th and early 16th centuries until an endowment by a local benefactor in 1565 made them unnecessary. They were re-introduced for the new bridge but were formally abolished with a grand procession and firework display on 12 March 1870.

24. Kingston Bridge before the tramways were built, *c*.1900. The tramways required substantial improvements to be made to many of the roads in Kingston, including the bridge, which was widened in 1914 to accommodate increased traffic.

25. The first 'Kingston' station at Surbiton, *c*.1838. This was a small cottage-like building on the south side of the line near the Ewell Road Bridge, which was approached by a path from the south end of the bridge down the cutting. It was opened on 21 May 1838 after a trial run on 12 May.

26.   Surbiton Station in 1902. The small station erected in 1838 soon became inadequate and a new one, on land given by Surbiton's first developer Thomas Pooley, was erected in 1840. It was rebuilt on the same site in 1938.

27.   Kingston Railway Station in 1863, designed by John Strapp. The railway bridge taking the line over the Thames to the station was designed by John Errington and was constructed by Brassey and Company. The extension to the line in 1869 altered the appearance of the original station and caused the break up of the rural Canbury Lodge Estate over which it passed. The station was rebuilt again in 1934.

28.   Commuters at Coombe and Malden Railway Station in 1908.

"NEW TIMES"
GUILDFORD & LONDON COACH

BOX SEAT	COACH-MAN		
GUILDFORD			
4	3	2	1
AND			
5	6	7	8
LONDON			
Guard	11	10	9

Coach by Messrs. HOLLAND & HOLLAND, 479 Oxford Street, W

❧ ❧ ❧

Messrs. Wimbush & Co., Ltd.,
Proprietors of the
"NEW TIMES" COACH
HALKIN STREET, GROSVENOR PLACE
LONDON, S.W.

Printers: The Garrick Press, 6, Henrietta St., W.C.

CALLING AT THE HYDE PARK HOTEL

COACHING SEASON
ON AND AFTER 1ST MAY

THE "NEW TIMES"
GUILDFORD & LONDON

PHOTO: W. A. ROUCH

WILL LEAVE THE
HOTEL VICTORIA, NORTHUMBERLAND AVENUE
EVERY DAY (SUNDAYS EXCEPTED)
AT 10.25 A.M.
RETURNING FROM THE
LION HOTEL, GUILDFORD
AT 3.10 P.M.
ARRIVING IN LONDON AT 6.30 P.M.

FARES

SINGLE - 10/-   RETURN - 15/-
Box Seat - 2/6 extra each way.
The whole of the Coach to Guildford and back, £8 8 0
Passengers' Luggage Free -:- -:- *Parcels carried and punctually delivered.*
Coach Booking Office: HOTEL VICTORIA, LONDON (Telephone 3984 Gerrard),
or at the LION HOTEL, GUILDFORD.

Messrs. WIMBUSH & CO., LTD., PROPRIETORS
For further particulars apply to
Halkin Street, Grosvenor Place, LONDON, S.W.

CALLING AT THE HYDE PARK HOTEL

THE "NEW TIMES" COACH TIME TABLE

DOWN
DAILY, SUNDAY EXCEPTED

Leave		Mileage
10.25	London, "Hotel Victoria"	
10.55	Hammersmith Broadway ..	4½
11.20	*Roehampton, "The King's Head" ..	8½
11.45	Kingston, "The Griffin"	11½
—	Thames Ditton	—
12.15	*Esher, "The Bear"	15½
—	Fair Mile	—
12.35	Cobham, "The White Lion"	19
—	Wisley Heath "The Hut"	21
1.05	*Ripley, "The Talbot"	23
1.40 Arrive	Guildford, "The Lion"	29

UP
DAILY, SUNDAY EXCEPTED

Leave		Mileage
3.10	Guildford, "The Lion"	
3.50	*Ripley, "The Talbot"	6
—	Wisley Heath, "The Hut" ..	8
4.15	Cobham, "The White Lion".. ..	10
—	Fair Mile	—
4.45	*Esher, "The Bear"	13½
	(Ten Minutes for Tea)	
—	Thames Ditton	—
5.10	Kingston, "The Griffin"	17½
5.40	*Roehampton, "The King's Head" ..	20½
—	Hammersmith Broadway ..	24½
6.30 Arrive	London, "Hotel Victoria"	29

Through Fare - - Fifteen Shillings

Intermediate Fares are charged at 4d. per mile, but not less than 1s. taken
* Change Horses   ♨ ♨ ♨ ♨   * Change Horses

CONVENIENT TRAINS FOR UP COACH
12.45 p.m. from Waterloo arrives Guildford at 1.28 p.m.

---

29. Timetable for the 'New Times' Coach, Guildford to London, late 19th century. A large number of coaches regularly visited Kingston earlier in the century bearing such attractive names as the 'Duke of Richmond', the 'Independent', the 'Express', the 'Union', the 'Royal Sussex', the 'Diligent', and the 'Rockett'. Most of them, including the 'New Times', stopped at the *Griffin* in the Market Place, for many centuries a well-known coaching inn. Competition between rival companies no doubt increased the efficiency of the service, and by the late 19th century they were co-ordinating their times with those of the railways.

30. Kingston's welcome to the trams in 1906. The formal inauguration of the trams by the Mayor, Councillor H. C. Minnitt, was timed for 11.30 a.m. on Thursday 1 March 1906. The first cars started from various termini at 7.30 a.m. and at each place crowds were waiting for a ride. The Mayor, under the supervision of Sir Clifton Robinson, Managing Director of London United Tramways, drove the tram across the bridge and up Kingston Hill where it was in collision with two drays belonging to Hodgson's Kingston Brewery. Sir Clifton Robinson was injured but was able to continue the journey to Surbiton Station and Tolworth, back through Surbiton to Winters Bridge at Long Ditton and then home to Kingston.

31. A London General Omnibus Company horse bus on the Putney to Surbiton route in 1910.

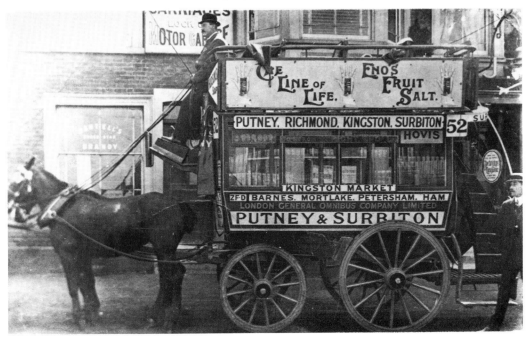

32. A motor outing for officers and staff of the Malden and Coombe Urban District Council on 13 June 1914. The chairman of the Highways Committee, who was soon to retire, invited 124 members of staff for an outing to Box Hill and the surrounding Surrey countryside. A fleet of motor charabancs lined up outside the Council offices in readiness for the day's excursion.

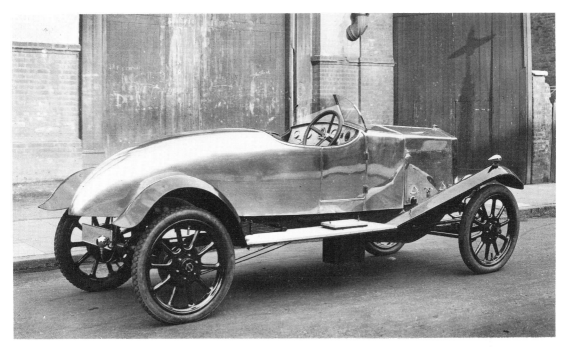

33. A car produced at the H. G. Hawker Engineering Company's works in Kingston. After the First World War aircraft production slowed down and the company began producing cars and motor cycles. This car, about which little is known, has just come off the production line judging by the lack of number plates.

34. The Kingston By-Pass Road in 1938. In the foreground are a number 152 bus, a Wolseley 14/56 and a Triumph 2-litre. The By-Pass, the first of its kind in the country, was opened in October 1927 by the Prime Minister, the Rt. Hon. Stanley Baldwin. The ceremony took place where the Merton spur joined the By-Pass. In his speech the Prime Minister made a plea for 'good roadside manners and no litter'.

Living in the Royal Borough

Daniel Defoe, visiting Kingston in the early 18th century on his 'tour through the whole island of Great Britain', found it a 'good market town but remarkable for little'. In contrast he was impressed by the scenes he encountered along the riverside between Richmond and London 'full of villages, beautiful buildings, charming gardens and rich habitations of quality'.

Before the railway developments of the 19th century the built-up area of Kingston centred on the Market Place and the streets radiating from it. Many of the poorer people lived in the squalid lanes north of the Market Place near the approach to the medieval bridge, while the more prosperous tradespeople, the maltsters for example, lived to the south. Norbiton, Surbiton, Malden and the area of modern New Malden were predominantly agricultural. Norbiton and Surbiton Commons provided open space around the town-centre which was not eroded until the Inclosure Commissioners allotted the land for development in 1838. In spite of Daniel Defoe's comments, Kingston could later also claim its fine mansions, extensive pleasure grounds, large estates and farms, notably the Coombe Estate, Norbiton Place, Woodbines House and Surbiton Place. Many were, however, destined to be depleted or demolished, and their lands built upon, in the post-railway rush for land in the 19th and early 20th centuries. Surbiton and New Malden were particularly affected. Their population had increased substantially upon the opening of their stations in 1838 and 1846 respectively and land for building was much sought after. Thomas Pooley and, later, Coutts Bank were active in Surbiton's development, whilst the National Freehold Land Society and other similar societies bought up estates in Kingston Hill, New Malden and Hook in order to build houses 'to enable men of small means to purchase freehold property to gain a vote'.

Farms and open land which had escaped development earlier fell to the developers in the 20th century, particularly in the 1920s and 1930s. Builders, encouraged by the opening of Kingston By-Pass, better communications and further railway extensions (for example, Berrylands Station in 1933 and the new Chessington line in 1939) were advertising comfortable Tudor-style homes like the Tudor estate off Richmond Road, convenient for both London and the countryside.

Alongside the ever-increasing number of privately developed estates were the Council houses built by local authorities under the Housing Acts. Kingston's earliest, the Cambridge Road Estate, was commenced in 1921 and was developed in several stages thereafter. These were followed by the post-Second World War estates such as the Mansfield Estate in Chessington, for which prisoner-of-war labour was used for the initial site clearance.

35. Norbiton House or Place, the property of Charles Nicholas Pallmer. This imposing residence (not to be confused with Norbiton Hall where the Earl of Liverpool's widow lived until her death in 1846) was owned by Pallmer in the early 19th century. Pallmer, who had made his money through sugar planting in the West Indies, was closely involved in the affairs of the town and was elected Member of Parliament for Surrey in 1826. He extended and improved the house and added more land to the estate which included farms, a large lake, a dairy in the style of an Indian temple and a grotto, totalling 300 acres in all. When Pallmer was bankrupted in 1836 the estate was sold in several lots. The mansion, which stood at the back of houses later to be built in Chatham Road, to the north-east of St Peter's church, fell into decline, but survived into the 20th century.

36. Woodbines House, also called Clock House, in 1906, just before its demolition. Woodbines House was an 18th-century mansion standing where the Portsmouth Road and Woodbines Avenue now meet. Parts of the estate were sold to Surrey County Council for County Hall in 1891 and 1905. The rest was sold for housing development in 1907 and 1908 to form Woodbines Avenue and Milner Road. In the 18th century the house belonged to Anna Barnard, the widow of a prominent Quaker, who diverted the Bittoms to its present position away from her pleasure garden. Owners in the 19th century included the Jemmett family, two members of which served as town clerks of Kingston. The house had been rebuilt in the early 18th century, possibly just after its use as a parish workhouse. Earlier, in the 17th century, the splendid park of the original house included an aviary, statues of Antony and Cleopatra, a lavish fountain and a vineyard.

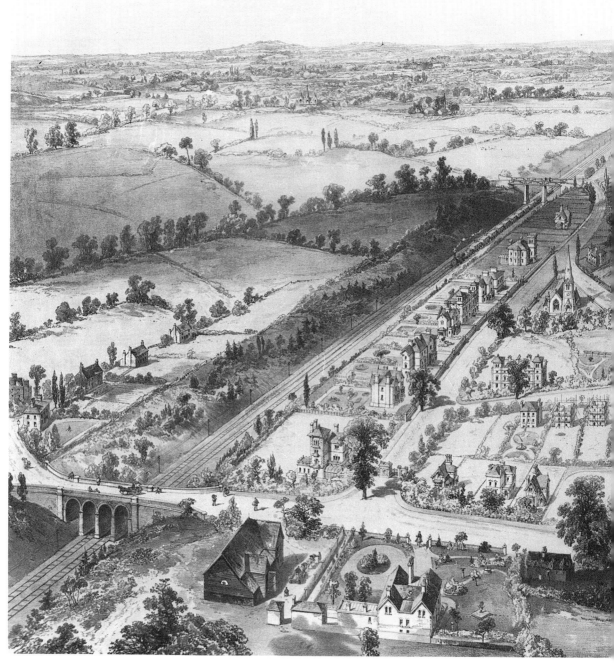

37. This bird's-eye view of Surbiton Hill Park (formerly called Selfe's Park) is remarkable for its detail. It probably dates from the third quarter of the 19th century and advertises 'highly eligible building property with the immediate surrounding respectable villa residences and beautiful extensive scenery'. Clearly visible are the present King Charles Road, Surbiton Hill Park, Parklands, Park Road, Regent Road and Berrylands, and in the distance, on the horizon, is the Crystal Palace.

38.   Hoppingwood Farm, New Malden, in 1900, one of the farms which surrounded Kingston before the major developments of the post-railway era. Comprising over 250 acres of arable and meadow, it was one of three large farms on the prestigious Coombe Estate purchased by the 1st Duke of Cambridge in 1837 from Earl Spencer. The farmhouse, demolished in 1911, stood roughly where Roseberry, Orchard, Hoppingwood and Alric Avenues were later built, and its lands are now partly Malden Golf Club and Beverley Park.

39.   Surbiton Place in the 19th century. The house was built in the 18th century by William Roffee and extended by the next owner, Thomas Fassett. Among its distinguished owners have been the Earl of Uxbridge (died 1812), his son, Henry William Paget, 1st Marquis of Anglesey (1768-1854) who sold the estate in 1817, John Garrett, a Kingston Councillor and Lord Mayor of London in 1824/25, and Alexander Raphael. Upon Raphael's death in 1850 much of the land was sold for development, and the names of the roads subsequently built reflect the names of previous owners. The house itself, standing on an island between Surbiton Crescent and Surbiton Road, was demolished in 1931.

40.   Berrylands Farm and dairy herd, Surbiton, *c*.1900. Berrylands and Berry Lodge Farms lay to the south of the railway line and extended, in the middle of the 19th century, from King Charles Road on the west to the Hogsmill River on the east and Tolworth to the south. The homestead, occupied by the Aspen family, was demolished in 1882 to make way for more building around the new Lawn Tennis Club. The farmhouse, often called Berry Lodge Farm, was occupied in the mid-19th century by another farmer, John Ablet, and stood just to the north of present Manor Crescent. It was demolished in 1930.

41.   View of Maple Road, Surbiton, in 1880, looking towards Brighton Road. In the distance, on the corner with Grove Road, is the Congregational church which was built in 1866 to replace an earlier one erected on the corner of St Leonard's Road in 1854. The latter was subsequently retained by the church as a schoolroom and still survives today as warehouse-offices. Town houses now stand on the site of the later church. Behind the cart on the right is Surbiton Crescent and opposite, just off the picture, is the turning into Claremont Road. Neither of the elegant mid-19th-century villas has survived. The far one has been replaced by flats. The near one, once called Sutherland House and used between 1884 and 1889 as a private asylum, and later by Crouch's the builders, was demolished in 1988 for a new office development.

42.   Interior view of Oak Hill Lodge, Oak Hill Grove, Surbiton, *c.*1890. This house still stands and is used as offices. In the late 19th century it was the gracious residence of Arthur Bryant (1841-84), brother of Wilberforce Bryant (of Bryant and May Matches, 1837-1906). Arthur's widow continued to live there after his death. Wilberforce had built himself a mansion in Surbiton in 1877 on the site of an older one and named it 'The Gables'. This also still stands. It later became the home of Sir Alfred Cooper, and is now Hillcroft College for Women in South Bank.

43a. The Cambridge Road Council Estate, Kingston's first under the 1919 Housing Act, was built in several phases from 1921. This is an example of one of the road lay-out plans prepared. They were eventually modified and simpler designs accepted.

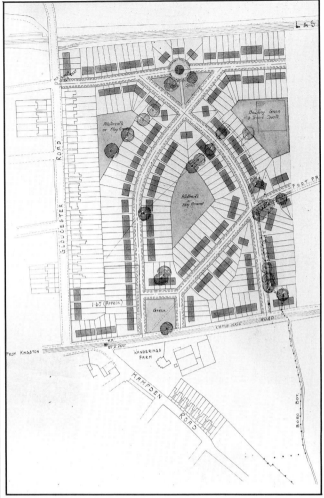

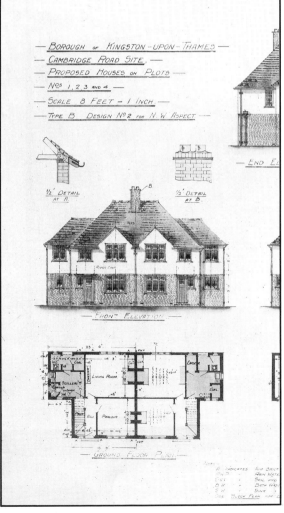

43b. A 1920 design for a Cambridge Road house – large compared with later council houses and built to high standards of light and ventilation. The first houses were built in 1921 on the corner of Gloucester Road and Cambridge Road.

43c. Building works at Norbiton Common Road looking toward King Henry's Road from Fleetwood Road, 1929.

43d. Fleetwood Road looking towards the railway, 1929.

44. Advertisement in the *Surrey Comet* for the Tudor Estate in Kingston, 1933. 'Local builders to work on historic lines. A great new "Tudor" estate will be developed on the Kingston to Richmond Road.' These were the headlines in the *Surrey Comet* for 18 November 1933. The advertisement extols the advantages of Crouch's new estate which had by then become familiar to home-buyers attending a recent Ideal Home Exhibition. 'Gables, half-timbering, lattice windows, plaster work' bore witness to a revival of interest in all things 'Tudor'. As for the interiors, however, 'modern architecture has shown how to use effectively every foot of space, and modern devices are employed at every turn to save labour'.

Schooldays and Beyond

Kingston Grammar School received its foundation charter from Elizabeth I in 1561 but there is documentary evidence for the existence of a school in Kingston as early as the 13th century. In the Middle Ages schools were often associated with religious foundations and Kingston's medieval school, perhaps a predecessor of the Elizabethan one, was associated with the chantry chapel of St Mary Magdalene in London Road. Erected in 1309 by Edward Lovekyn, a Bailiff of Kingston, and rebuilt in 1352, the Foundation was abolished and its endowments confiscated at the Reformation. It is significant that in granting lands for the maintenance of the 'new' Grammar School in 1561 and 1564 Queen Elizabeth included the Lovekyn Chapel as part of its endowment. The Bailiffs of Kingston became the governors and two schoolwardens were appointed annually to administer the funds. Famous scholars have included the historian Edward Gibbon (1737-94) and the playwright R. C. Sherriff (1896-1975).

Poor children in the Borough were educated by charity money bequeathed by private individuals, among them Thomas and John Tiffin whose bequests (1638-39) enabled 'honest poor men's sons' to be taught 'in some good school to write, read and cast accompt'. Other children, distinguished by their variously coloured uniforms, were educated under the bequests of Mrs. Elizabeth Brown (1648) and Edward Belitha (1717).

Encouraged, no doubt, by the Sunday School movement of the late 18th century, a Sunday School was opened in 1798 in Brick Lane (later called Union Street), and others connected with both Anglican and Nonconformist churches followed. There were also many local private or 'dame' schools in the area.

Concern over the education of poor children in Kingston in the 19th century resulted in the establishment, in 1818, of a 'Public School' in the Richmond Road which was funded by 'donation, loan and public subscription'. The early years of the 19th century also saw the emergence of the National Society for Promoting the Education of the Poor (Anglican) and the British and Foreign Schools Society (Nonconformist). As a result many National Schools were established in the area, among them, in 1838, St Peter's, Norbiton (later St Peter's Church of England School).

The Ragged School Movement, championed by Anthony Ashley Cooper, Earl of Shaftesbury (1801-85), influenced the opening of a Ragged School in Old Bridge Street in 1853 'to mitigate the utter and deplorable ignorance which prevailed among the gutter children of the back lanes'.

In 1874 the Endowed Schools Commission produced a scheme for the establishment of 'lower middle class' schools in Kingston. Under the scheme, many of the old educational charities were amalgamated, among them the Tiffin Charity. The Tiffin Schools as we know them today were founded and, subsequently, they and the Grammar School were administered together by a board of governors which included members of the Corporation.

Attendance at school was not compulsory until 1876 when the employment of children under ten became illegal. A school attendance officer for Kingston was appointed to 'attend the public streets four hours each day ... with a view to ascertaining what children do not attend school'.

A Borough Education Committee was established in 1903 under the Balfour Education Act but in 1944 (under the Education Act of that year) Surrey County Council assumed responsibility for most of the schools in the Borough, with the exception of Kingston

Grammar School which became a Direct Grant School. The newly-enlarged Borough became its own Education Authority in 1965. The Grammar School is now an Independent School.

45a. & b. 'Blue' and 'Green' charity children in Kingston, 1826. The charity children looked distinctive in their blue, green and brown uniforms. They were required to appear regularly before the Bailiffs of the town 'with their books to see how they write'. In 1828 they received a dinner of roast beef and plum pudding to celebrate the opening of the new bridge, and, before the bridge was made toll-free, they were permitted to cross it free of charge.

46. Kingston Public School, Richmond Road, in 1907. A 'public' school for the education of poor children, funded by local subscription, was established in Kingston in 1818. The picture shows the original school buildings. In 1878 a school inspector commented on the efficiency of the teaching and discipline but criticised the furniture and apparatus. 'The desks were old and shaky, the rooms badly warmed and there was only a shed at the other side of the playground for cloaks and hats.' The school was rebuilt in 1907 and the buildings survive today as an annexe of Kingston College of Further Education.

47. St Peter's School, Norbiton, c.1907. The slate held by the boy in the front row reads 'Class VI'. Norbiton National School (later St Peter's Church of England Primary School) was opened in 1838 as an infants' school for children under the age of eight, and was managed by a committee of ladies. By the time the school moved to new buildings in Cambridge Road in 1853, older children were admitted and there were separate departments for boys, girls and infants. The school closed in 1960 but the buildings have survived.

48. The boys of St Peter's, Norbiton, enjoying a game of playground cricket, *c*.1908.

49. **Children from St Paul's National School, Hook, *c*.1900. The school, built on the corner of Hook Road and Orchard Road, was opened in 1860.**

50.   Bonner Hill School, *c.*1906. The school, built between Oil Mill Lane (modern Villiers Road) and Bonner Hill Road, was opened in 1906 with total accommodation for 1,142 children – 398 infants, 372 boys and 372 girls. The Borough Education Committee claimed that the buildings met 'all modern requirements, each department being well lighted, heated and ventilated, with a spacious central hall, eight classrooms, teachers' rooms, cloakrooms, lavatories, a covered playshed and a large asphalted playground'. The school closed in 1980 and houses now occupy the site.

51. The weekly competition of summer flowers at Bonner Hill School in 1908. Gardening and nature study classes were an important part of the curriculum and, soon after the school was built, a small garden was laid out next to the infants' school for the children to tend.

52.　A drawing class in progress at Bonner Hill School in 1908.

53a. & b.   Empire Day celebrations at Bonner Hill School in 1922.

54.   A Kingston Grammar School class, *c.*1908/9. The playwright, R. C. Sherriff, was educated at Kingston Grammar School. This class photograph, from amongst his papers, may have been taken about 1908/9 when he was 12 or 13 years of age (possibly middle row, third from back). The classroom now forms part of the school's music room.

55.   The Knox Guild of Design and Craft: a demonstration of pottery by Denise Tuckfield (later Wren) in the art gallery of Kingston Library, now the Heritage Centre, *c.*1913. The potter's wheel had been purchased from Mr. Mercer, flower pot maker, in Norbiton in 1912. In that year Denise and fellow students from Kingston School of Art founded the Knox Guild to continue the teachings of their design master, Alexander Knox. The aim of the Guild, the headquarters of which were at 24 Market Place, Kingston, was to encourage the development of English handicrafts and design. The founder members, mostly women, wore overalls embroidered in the suffragette colours. Denise and her husband, Henry Wren, whom she married in 1915, founded the Oxshott Potteries in 1920.

SURREY EDUCATION COMMITTEE.

TIFFIN'S GIRLS' SCHOOL, KINGSTON.

E.S.A. LONDON. *Copyright.*

Never Absent, Never Late

56. 'Never absent, never late' postcard. Rewards for regular attendance were given to school children by the Surrey Education Committee in the form of picture postcards, certificates and medals. The postcards depicted a variety of local scenes. This one illustrates Tiffin Girls' School which formerly stood on the corner of Penrhyn Road and Kingston Hall Road. The buildings were afterwards occupied by the School of Art and Technical Institute, later Kingston College of Further Education.

57. Hillcroft College for Women, South Bank, Surbiton. This 'Residential College for Working Women' was established in Beckenham in 1920 and moved in 1926 to 'The Gables', Surbiton, the former home of Wilberforce Bryant and Sir Arthur Cooper. The original aim of the college, renamed Hillcroft upon its arrival in Surbiton, was to offer a 'second chance' to women who were 'educationally deprived'. The college still operates successfully today.

The Working Day

Many of Kingston's early industries were influenced by its position on the River Thames and by its success as an important market town serving northern Surrey.

Archaeological evidence for pottery kilns in Eden Street in the Middle Ages bears witness to an important trade which occasionally supplied the royal household with consignments of pottery, whilst the survival into later times of the field name 'tenterfield' – where the cloth was stretched – suggests that Kingston once supported some kind of wool trade.

Kingston's position as an important market town encouraged another industry. Cattle would be brought to market on the hoof and slaughtered locally. A by-product of the meat trade would have been hides, and the famous Kingston tannery in Thames Street – well known for its odour – survived until a fire gutted its buildings in 1963. Another associated industry was tallow-chandlery. Candles made from fat were manufactured at Ranyard's in the Market Place near the tannery. The business under the ownership of W. G. Smith moved to St James' Road in the 1850s and then, around 1895, to the old linseed oil mills in Oil Mill Lane (modern Villiers Road). A *Surrey Comet* reporter visiting the factory in 1901 reported 'the absence of offensive odours and the clean and tidy appearance of men and boys employed there'. Another mill on the Hogsmill River, used for corn milling and known as Marsh's in the 19th century, later became the headquarters of Johnston's 'yewsabit' polish works, and was demolished to make way for the Coronation Baths in Denmark Road in 1936. The sites of the mills are now covered by an industrial estate and new housing respectively.

As a riverside town Kingston was a centre of the fishing trade. It has also traditionally been associated with brewing and malting, industries which relied heavily on river transport for supplies. Alderman Gould who came to the town in 1839 remarked that 'Kingston was then a celebrated malting town; there were malthouses visible in all directions and everywhere one turned there were Inland Revenue Officers'. Hodgson's, one of Kingston's well-known breweries (later Courage's), stood on a site between St James' Road and Brook Street until its destruction in 1971.

Turks, the boat builders, and the name of Kingston are synonymous. This famous business has been a feature of Kingston's riverside from the mid-18th century. Their boats have been prize winners at a number of international exhibitions, including the Great Exhibition of 1885 in London, and members of both English and foreign royal houses are numbered amongst past patrons. Queen Victoria, for example, placed orders for boats for use on the Home Park Waters and at garden parties at Buckingham Palace, where members of the Turk family officiated as Queen's Watermen.

At the beginning of the 20th century Kingston was rapidly expanding into a small but important manufacturing and light industrial centre encouraged by the opening of Kingston By-Pass where many factories began to open their doors. Some of the well-known traditional businesses, as well as lesser-known family ones, are illustrated in this section, as is the former Sopwith Aviation Company, later Hawker's (now British Aerospace), which perhaps did most to put Kingston on the industrial map at the beginning of the present century.

58. Kingston Workmen's Club and Institute in Fairfield Road, *c.*1878. The club, established in 1878, was affiliated to the Working Men's Club and Institute Union whose headquarters were in the Strand. Its objects were 'to promote the social and intellectual welfare of the working men of Kingston and neighbourhood'. The accommodation consisted of reading and smoking rooms, a large club room for concerts and entertainments, a library, recreation room and gymnasium. Connected with the Institute were bicycle, cricket and rowing clubs. In July 1908 the foundation stone of a new building was laid in London Road and this building was vacated. It was later used by the Salvation Army.

59. The old Oil Mill in Oil Mill Lane (modern Villiers Road), *c.*1900-1910. Originally called Chapel Mill because it once belonged to the Lovekyn Chapel, the mill later became known as Oil Mill to reflect its use, from the 18th century, for the production of linseed oil. The buildings were purchased in 1895 by W. G. Smith for the manufacture of candles – a business he had taken over from the Ranyard family whose tallow-chandlery in the Market Place was well known. After Smith's death the mill was purchased in 1922 by Prices, the candle firm. Today an industrial estate stands on the site, but the mill house has survived.

60. The 'new' offices of Knapp Drewett, proprietors of the *Surrey Comet*, in Clarence Street, 1906. The *Surrey Comet* started life in 1854 in Brighton Road, Surbiton, and later moved to a house near Kingston Bridge. In 1863 the proprietor built new premises at 20 Clarence Street. In 1907, these were demolished to make way for new offices, the elegant frontages of which still remain in Clarence Street today. In 1927 the newspaper moved once again, this time to a Tudor-style building in Church Street (now the site of Mothercare and a new shopping complex). The newspaper now operates from offices in the Lower Ham Road.

61. H. Vining, tobacco-pipe maker, at his bench, *c*.1931. The Vinings were a Kingston family of tobacconists and pipe makers whose business in Park Road dates back to at least 1862. Kingston Heritage Centre has a complete set of Mr. Vining's moulds and pipes.

62a. & b.   Advertisement for Hodgson's Ales, 1891, and a brewery delivery van in 1914. Hodgson's Brewery occupied an extensive site between Brook Street and St James' Road. It was originally owned by the Rowlls family whose mansion, Kingston Hall, stood next to the brewery. The brewery was acquired by the Hodgson family in 1854, and was taken over by Courage's in 1943. Brewing ceased in 1951 and the buildings became a bottling plant until 1965 when they were closed down altogether. They were destroyed by fire in 1971 and an office and shopping complex now occupies the site.

63. A group of workmen at the Kingston Tannery, *c.*1930. The Tannery in Thames Street, on the riverside, was an old-established Kingston business dating back to the late 18th century. The site consiste of over 230 pits which contained hides in various stages of manufacture. The chief material in the preparation of leather was oak-bark, a principal source of tannin. In 1963 the business closed and the buildings, in the process of being demolished, were destroyed by a massive fire in June 1963.

64. Richard Turk (right), of the firm of R. J. Turk & Sons, boatbuilders, waterman to King George V, c.1910.

65a. The Sopwith Aviation Company's buildings in Canbury Park Road. In 1912 Sir Thomas Sopwith established the Sopwith Aviation Company in Kingston in an old roller-skating rink in Canbury Park. In 1914 additional factory accommodation was built in Canbury Park Road and Richmond Road. The latter, leased in 1928 for 20 years to Leyland Motors, is now the headquarters of British Aerospace in Kingston. The Canbury Park building is currently (1989) used by Kingston Polytechnic. The building looks much the same today except for the loss of the surrounding wall. The little white building beyond the chimney was the Design Office. In 1913 the Company employed six fitter/carpenters and a tea-boy, and the templates for the aircraft were often drawn out on the floors in chalk.

65b. Sopwith 'Dolphins' in production at the Canbury Park Road factory. The limited size of the building meant that most of the mass-production was done at Richmond Road or contracted out to other companies.

66. A Sopwith Baby Float Plane in 1912 on the Thames at Kingston where flight trials were a common sight and provoked great local interest. The Thames Conservancy was not so amused and complained when the river was used as a runway.

67. The 'dope' shop at the aircraft works, *c.*1939-42. The women are seen applying a kind of varnish to the surfaces of the tail planes which made them rigid and gave them their aerodynamic quality. The lacquer or 'dope' was so pungent that the women were issued with half a pint of milk a day which, they claimed, helped to counteract the effects of the fumes. The planes being assembled are Hawker Hurricanes.

68. G. T. Jones & Company, photographic artists and miniature painters, *c.*1900-1910. Messrs. G. T. Jones acquired this old established photographic firm at 9 Surbiton Park Terrace around 1883. They were patronised by Queen Victoria and the Prince of Wales and took photographs of many other distinguished people of the day, including the Duchess of Albany and the Duchess of Wellington. They recorded for posterity many important local events, including the opening of Kingston's Sewage Works, and during the Boer War they took photographs of the Gables Hospital at Surbiton to be presented as souvenirs to the wounded soldiers.

69a. & b.   Mrs. Mollie Surman, artificial eye maker, *c.*1950. Mrs. Surman carried on her business as a glass eye maker in Thames Street, Kingston, from 1943 and later moved to a house in the Ewell Road, Surbiton. The artificial eye business had been a family concern – her father practised in London – and Mollie made her first eye at the age of twelve. Her workshop was modest – all she needed were a workbench, glass and blow lamp. Many of the eyes were made to order and famous personalities have been numbered among her clients. She also treated servicemen wounded during the Second World War.

70.   Potteries and brickworks in Blagdon Road, Norbiton, *c.*1900-1910, established in 1877 by Benjamin Looker, junior, whose family had been brickmakers and potters in Kingston from the early 19th century. The potteries survived until the Second World War when the pits were taken over by Malden and Coombe Urban District Council for a rubbish tip.

71a. The packing department of C. R. (Cleanliness and Regularity) Laundry in Cavendish Road, *c.*1938. The New Malden branch of the C. R. laundry was established in 1912 by Mr. W. T. Wild who lived at Blagdon Road and, later, Malden Road. His daughter, Phyllis, worked in the business from 1913, at first doing inside jobs and, during the First World War, driving a horse-drawn delivery van around the district. Later she became manager of over 80 staff. The Laundry could boast many famous clients including General Eisenhower who occupied Telegraph Cottage on Kingston Hill during the Second World War. The Laundry closed in 1964.

71b. A fleet of vans used by the C. R. Laundry in 1938. The van in front, a three-wheeler 'special', was used to transport urgent (and costly) deliveries. In 1939 the fleet was commandeered by the army and the laundry had to borrow or hire others until their own were released. The Laundry's fleet of horses, which pulled the wagons before 1919/20, was similarly commandeered during the First World War.

Shopping

Kingston Market Place, located near the river, bridge and ancient parish church, has been a familiar landmark from medieval times. With a Town Hall (now the Market House) at its centre, it has formed the hub of Kingston's civic and commercial life for centuries. There is evidence that the market was flourishing in the 13th century and many of Kingston's charters relate to market and fair rights granted to the town by successive monarchs. Market trading was governed by four trading companies: the Woollen Drapers, Mercers, Shoemakers and Butchers. Traders in the town were enrolled as freemen of one of the four companies either by right of patrimony or after serving an apprenticeship.

Those who were not Freemen, often called 'foreigners', encountered many restrictions and were allowed to trade in the town only on payment of a 'fine'. This was generally a money payment but it was occasionally paid in kind. In 1739, for example, a cutler provided the Corporation with silver-plated cutlery in return for his right to bring his wares to town. Such restrictions were ended by the municipal reforms of the early 19th century.

A livestock market was originally held in the Market Place but was moved to the Fairfield in 1925. This finally closed for the sale of animals in 1957 and developed into a general goods market (the Monday Market) which is still very popular today.

The market stalls were originally only temporary structures which were dismantled at the end of each market day. The area surrounding the Market Place was, however, a prime site for shopkeepers and its present shape was probably established early by traders who replaced their temporary stalls with permanent buildings. It is not surprising that with much of Kingston's trading taking place there, shopkeepers and stall holders viewed with alarm an abortive suggestion by the Council in 1837 to build the Town Hall elsewhere, fearing that much of their trade would disappear.

Kingston's first 'department' store, a pioneer of its kind, was situated to the west of the Market Place, next to the *Sun Inn*, later to become Woolworths. Known variously over the years as Clarkson, Knight and Pratt, Shrubsole's, Hide's and Chiesmans, it began life in 1740, extended its premises in the 19th century to include the *Castle Inn*, and ended life as the Army and Navy Store (1983-87). Now (1988-89) used for temporary shop units, the site is scheduled for the Charter Quay redevelopment.

It was probably not until the 19th century that the shopping area spread to any significant extent to other parts of Kingston. Outlying regions like Surbiton and Norbiton were relatively rural and it was not until the advent of the railways that other areas away from the town centre proper were developed. Victoria Road and Electric Parade (later Brighton Road), for example, became the shopping areas for Surbiton which grew rapidly after the railways arrived in 1838.

No study of shopping in Kingston would be complete without reference to Bentall's, Kingston's well-known department store. Started in 1867 by Frank Bentall, it rapidly expanded along Wood Street and Clarence Street, receiving a major face-lift in 1935 with a now-familiar facade designed by Maurice Webb. Major reconstruction of this store began again in 1987 and, opposite, a new John Lewis store is under construction, continuing the trend for bigger all-encompassing stores begun in a small way by Clarkson, Knight and Pratt in the 18th century.

72. George Day, second-hand furniture dealer and cutler, in the Horse Fair in 1894. The area of Kingston known as the Horse Fair, north of the Market Place, is now the site of the John Lewis development.

73a. The Saturday Market in Kingston Market Place, *c.*1897. This view of Kingston's busy Market Place, which still retains its ancient shape, looks south towards the Hogsmill river and Clattern Bridge. On the left is the old Town Hall later called the Market House, the ground floor of which is still occupied by small shops. On the right of the picture is the *Sun Inn* which became part of Woolworths in 1931, and next to it is Hide's, Kingston's first department store.

73b. The Cattle Market in the Market Place at Kingston, *c.*1907. The right to hold a Saturday cattle market was granted to Kingston by James I in 1603 but cattle trading had been a feature of Kingston's markets long before this date. In 1855 livestock day became Thursday and eventually, because of overcrowding in the Market Place, a substitute cattle and goods market on a Monday was opened in the Fairfield in 1925.

1887. Will commence on Saturday, the FIRST of JANUARY, and continue till the FIRST of FEBRUARY.

29 & 31, THAMES STREET, KINGSTON-ON-THAMES.

1870

POWELL & COMPY LONDON BRANCH.

F. POWELL. CLOTHIER OUTFITTER F. POWELL. & DRAPER.

[11]

F. Powell & Co.'s Great Annual Sale.

Mechanics' Clothing

DEPARTMENT.

The principal feature in this Department is DURABILITY and STRENGTH.

WE SHALL MAKE SOME

☞ GREAT REDUCTIONS IN THE PRICE OF OUR NOTED CORD TROUSERS.☜

MEN'S.—150 pairs BEST QUALITY   6/11 usual price 8/11 Special

Some Special Jobs at 3/11½ pair—Men's Special

☞ A STRONG USEFUL TROUSERS, in Lemon, Drab, White and Smoke Cord, Rule Pocket, Bell Bottoms, 3/11 and 5/11 per pair

Men's Cord Vests 2/11½ 3/6 3/11   Men's Cord and Mole Wellsinker Vests 6/11 8/11
Black and White Check Wellsinker Vests 8/9
Worsted Cord Trousers 8/11 12/11 14/11   White Mole Trousers 3/11 4/11 6/11

Coalheavers' Slops   .   1/0½ each--SPECIAL JOB

DRABBET JACKETS   DUCK JACKETS   HOLLAND BLOUSES

ENGINEERS' CLOTHITG.

Blue Dungaree Jackets ... ... 2/11   Blue Serge Trousers 2/6
Blue Dungaree Trousers ... ... 2/11   Blue Serge Jackets ... 2/11 3/11 4/9

BUTCHERS' CLOTHING.

BLUE JEAN SLOPS. BLUE TWILL COATS. SERGE APRONS, 1/0½ 1/6½ 1/9½ 1/11½

Notice to Watermen!

F. POWELL & Co. can supply OILSKIN COATS of the very BEST Quality at the LOWEST possible Prices.—SOU'-WESTERS from 1/4½ each

LEGGINGS.

MACINTOSH LEGGINGS 3/11½ 4/9
BOYS' PATENT LEGGINGS ... ... 1/11½ SPECIAL
YOUTHS' PATENT LEGGINGS ... ... 2/6 SPECIAL
MEN'S PATENT LEGGINGS 3/6 4/11
MEN'S PATENT MACINTOSH TOP LEGGINGS 6/6
MEN'S TAN RIDING LEGGINGS 2/3 3/11 4/11 6/11 8/6
MEN'S BROWN COWHIDE LEGGINGS 5/11 6/6
MEN'S HIDE NAPOLEON LEGGINGS 3/11 4/11
MEN'S HIDE WELLINGTON LEGGINGS 4/11
YOUTHS' PATENT NAPOLEON LEGGINGS, with Tongues 3/6
MEN'S „   „   „   „ 3/11
MEN'S BROWN PATENT LEGGINGS, Extra Quality 5/11
Boys' and Men's Tan and Hide Leggings—ALL PRICES.

A Job Lot of Boys' Leggings from 6d. pair

From 1st JANUARY till 1st FEBRUARY, 1887.

74a. & b.   Advertisements for F. Powell's annual sale in 1887. By the date of this sale catalogue, F. Powell, clothier, outfitter and draper, had occupied 19-31 Thames Street (west side) for some years. The date on the roof of the building reads 1870. The catalogue advertises a wide range of items from their many departments, including linens, corsetry, children's clothes, curtaining, hosiery, millinery, and boots and shoes. The store was taken over in the 1890s by Weeks and Venn (later Austin Venn) who were also drapers and outfitters and whose china department stood opposite in Clarence Street.

WRIGHT BROS., LTD., KINGSTON.
SALE of AFTERNOON FROCKS & EVENING GOWNS
SUITABLE FOR CHRISTMAS, at RIDICULOUS PRICES,
TO-DAY & DURING NEXT WEEK.

We have only one of each of these gowns that are illustrated, but hold a large selection of equally dainty garments at similar reductions. A visit to our showrooms we are confident will repay you.

Having purchased a stock of CONY SEAL COATS at a big Discount for Cash, we are offering same at exceptional sale prices this week from 4½gns. to 12gns.

Evening Gown in White Charmeuse with handsome Pink Embroidered Tunic. Usual Price 4½ gns.
Sale Price 2gns.

(1) **Smart Afternoon Frock** in Eolienne Silk with Pleated Tunic and Lace Front.
Sale Price £4 4s.

(2) **Charming Frock** in Black Charmeuse Silk. Usual Price 6½gns.
Sale Price 2 gns.

(3) **Black Velveteen Gown**, Bodice and Tunic edged Fur. Usual price 3gns.
Sale Price 2 gns.

(4) **Dainty Frock** in heavy Mole Crepe Silk. Bodice and Flounces of Palon Charmeuse. Usual Price 6½gns.

Model Evening Gown in Pink Glace Silk, skirt heavily beaded in grey and pink. Usual price 15gns.
Sale Price 5gns.

75. Advertisement in the *Surrey Comet* for Wright Brothers' sale in 1914. Wright Brothers, variously described as milliners, hosiers and fancy drapers, had premises near Powell's at numbers 17 and 23-25 Thames Street. In 1910 they took over Powell's old shop and in 1914/15 relinquished numbers 23-25 to Lyons, Caterers. They remained in Thames Street until 1930 when their store was taken over by Wolfe and Hollander.

76. Messrs. H. Linton & Co., butchers in Church Street, Kingston, 1897. Linton's set up in business in 1833 and occupied a corner shop in Church Street, close to the Market Place and the parish church. According to an illustrated trades directory of 1891 their shop always had a clean and attractive appearance and was 'provided with all the fittings and accessories necessary for the rapid dispatch of a large and high-class trade'. The photograph shows two of their four horse-drawn vans which made daily deliveries to all parts of the neighbourhood. The building is now occupied by Thornton's confectionery shop.

77. E. M. Taylor, 'wardrobe dealer' in Union Street, c.1910. This small shop, number 11a, stood on the west side of Union Street and was owned, along with number 11, by Miss E. M. Taylor and two other members of the family, Edward Taylor and Walter James Taylor, for a few years up to and including the First World War. The site of the building is now covered by Crown Arcade.

78a. & b.   The Home and Colonial Stores in Clarence Street, Kingston, in the 1920s. This shop had been established by Julius Drew who, at the age of 17, had joined the firm of Francis Peek and Winch, tea-importers, which had been established in Liverpool by his mother's brother, Francis Peek. At a time when the first multiple stores were being started, Drew opened his first shop in 1878 in Liverpool, and in 1883 moved to London with his new partner, John Musker. The business developed into the Home and Colonial Stores and made Drew and Musker rich men. By the early 1890s Kingston had its first Home and Colonial at 41 Market Place and by 1909 another branch had been established at 26 Clarence Street. By the mid-1950s number 26 had been incorporated into an extended Marks and Spencer Store.

79.   Victoria Road, Surbiton's main shopping street, looking towards Brighton Road, *c*.1910.
The shop to the right in the foreground of the picture was M. Griggs which occupied numbers
1 and 2, 4 and 5 as a drapers, ladies' outfitters and furnishing store. To the left foreground, just off
the picture, is the railway station. In 1910 over 90 traders and professional people occupied
premises along the road and at number 56 the Kingston, Surbiton and District Fire Brigade had
an engine house.

80.   Bentall's at the corner of Clarence Street and Wood Street, *c*.1899. Bentall's, established in
1867 in Clarence Street, gradually extended to take in properties round the corner into Wood
Street including, in 1919, the Tudor-style vicarage of 1855 which became the store's Tudor
Restaurant. Opposite, the old mansion called Down Hall was purchased for the site of an indoor
car park. In 1899 the *Red Lion* public house and All Saints' Church School and Mission Hall (seen
in the photograph) were purchased, enabling the store to accomplish a unified façade. The
Tudor part of the building was demolished in 1988 and a new Bentall's store at the back of the
present building is in the course of construction in 1988/89.

81a. & b.   Women at Sopwith's aircraft factory making toy crocodiles in 1919. The end of the hostilities in 1918 meant that the Sopwith factory could turn its hand to other mechanical inventions. These clockwork crocodiles, seen here in production at the Company's factory in Kingston, were destined for Bentall's toy department for the Christmas trade. The 'Kingston Crocodiles' and the 'Toyland Pug' were advertised, along with other children's toys, in the December 1919 issue of the *Surrey Comet*.

82a. & b. H. C. Webb, butcher, Cambridge Road, Norbiton, in the 1920s. The Webbs were an old established firm of family butchers with several branches. Directories for the early part of the century list them at Excelsior Road, Cambridge Grove Road and Cambridge Road, and their van, pictured below, advertised H. C. Webb & Sons at Norbiton, Kingston Market Place, and across the river at Hampton Wick. Harry Charles Webb appears in the directories at the Cambridge Road premises (now Wizard Wine) from 1922 where the firm, by 1934 H. C. Webb & Sons, is listed until the late 1950s.

83a. & b. The shopping parade in Malden Road, New Malden (now High Street), *c.*1900 (*above*), and the opening of Woolworths in 1936 (*below*). Woolworths was built on part of the site of former doctors' premises known as 'Dunurlin', at a central position on Malden Road. The *Surrey Comet* called it an 'ultra-modern store'. The remainder of the site was developed at the same time as a parade of 'modern' shops and flats, to be called the Broadway Parade.

Worship

The present Royal Borough is served by many churches of all denominations, Anglican, Roman Catholic and Nonconformist. The latter include the Society of Friends and the United Reformed (formerly Congregational) churches, both in Eden Street, whose members were active in Kingston from the late 17th century. Originally gathering at private meeting houses, they suffered persecution under the Conventicle Acts of the 1660s and 1670s which lasted until the Toleration Act of 1689. The Baptist church in Union Street was founded in 1790 (its present building dates from 1864) and another, the Bunyan Baptist church in Queen Elizabeth Road, seceded from the Union Street church in 1882 (the present building was erected in 1977). There is evidence also for early 19th-century Methodist chapels in the town, for example in Canbury Fields (1836) and St James' Road (1862), both replaced by the Eden Street (Wesleyan) church in 1890. Alexander Raphael completed his private chapel, St Raphael's Roman Catholic church in the Portsmouth Road, in 1847.

Prior to the 19th century, Kingston's medieval church, All Saints', served a large parish. It was the social and religious centre for the people of Kingston and the outlying districts of Norbiton and Surbiton, just as the churches in Old Malden and Chessington served their own respective rural communities.

In 1842 the doors of a new parish church opened to an expanding community in Norbiton. St Peter's was the first of a number of new parishes carved out of the older ancient parishes, among them St Mark's in Surbiton (1845) and Christ Church, New Malden (1866). Many other churches of all denominations and creeds followed.

84a. All Saints', Kingston's ancient parish church, photographed about 1900. The existence of a church in Kingston is recorded in the Domesday Survey of 1086.

84b. Traces of Norman stonework were discovered in the church in 1858 and photographed before being removed during alteration work. The removal of the spire after damage caused by a hurricane in 1703 and substantial alterations to the fabric of the building over the centuries have changed its appearance considerably.

85. An interior view of All Saints', *c*.1840. A baptism is in progress.

86. The Vicarage House belonging to All Saints' church, *c.*1820. This house stood in Wood Street amid extensive gardens on part of the site now occupied by Bentall's Department Store. By the 1840s the vicar was living elsewhere in Eden Street, and the house was occupied by Miss Taylor, the parish church organist, who ran a school for young ladies there. The vicarage was rebuilt in 1855 by the architect S. S. Teulon and later formed part of Bentall's 'Tudor' entrance in Wood Street (demolished in 1988 to make way for a new Bentall's development).

87. Dedication and opening of the memorial gates at All Saints' church, by the Bishop of Kingston, Dr. Herbert, on Armistice Sunday, 9 November 1924. The gates were erected in memory of all ranks of the East Surrey Regiment who fell in the Great War. The other part of the memorial consisted of a chapel inside the church and a Book of Remembrance.

88. St Peter's church, Norbiton, in 1841. The
parish of St Peter's was the first to be created
from the large 'ancient' parish of Kingston.
Designed by Scott and Moffatt, the church was
dedicated and opened for worship in 1842.

89. The original church of St John the Baptist,
Kingston Vale. Prior to the building of the
church the vicar of Ham was responsible for the
inhabitants of Kingston Vale but bad roads and
poor communications meant they were unable
to attend the parish church regularly. This small
chapel was consecrated in 1847. It stood close to
the road on the same side as the present church
in what is now Mary Adelaide Close.

The original Church.
Built 1847, demolished 1862.
It stood close to the high-road, on the right of the church path, a few feet back.

90.   The present church of St John the Baptist, Kingston Vale. This was built on land given by the Duke of Cambridge and was consecrated in 1861. It was enlarged by the addition of a north aisle and organ chamber in 1874-75 and a new choir vestry in 1886.

91.   An unused design for St John the Baptist, Kingston Vale. This is what the church might have looked like had the plans of Francis Pougett been accepted. The design was presented to the church by Queen Mary in 1947.

92.   Princess Mary Adelaide, Duchess of Teck (died 1897), and her daughter, Princess May, later Queen
Mary, who resided at White Lodge and were regular worshippers at Kingston Vale.

93. Kingston Congregational church in Eden Street, *c*.1856. This church, built in 1856, replaced an earlier building erected on the same site in 1803. The first service in the new building was held on 9 July, after which the *Surrey Comet* commented 'everything in the church looks good and in excellent taste, but the gas is perhaps the most effective of all the internal arrangements'. The building was refurbished and extended by the addition of new halls in 1977.

94. The Rev. L. H. Byrnes, minister of Kingston Congregational church, 1851-69. During his ministry the Surbiton Park Congregational church (1866) and the Kingston church were built. The two churches were amalgamated in 1966.

95.   Bunyan Baptist Sunday School children in a coronation procession in Fife Road, Kingston, in 1902.

96. A view of Eden Street, c.1906, showing Kingston's Wesleyan Methodist church on the corner with Fairfield Road. Called the Victoria Jubilee Wesleyan church, it was designed by James Weir and built by William Johnson of Wandsworth. It was opened on 4 June 1890 to replace the St James' Road chapel. The church was demolished in 1964 and a new one built in Fairfield South in 1966.

97. St Mark's church, Surbiton, in the early years of this century. The parish of St Mark was the first of the new parishes in Surbiton to be created from the original 'ancient' parish of Kingston. The church, designed by Philip Hardwicke, was consecrated in 1845 and enlarged in 1854. It was almost entirely destroyed by enemy fire bombs on 20 October 1940. Services were subsequently held in a school hall and later in a temporary church in Church Hill Road, until the new church, begun in 1955, was consecrated in 1960.

98a. & b.   William Passey (1824-1904), London City
Missioner for Surbiton, and his second wife, Ann. William
started his career with the London City Mission in
Bloomsbury in 1849 where he taught in a Ragged School
above a blacksmith's shop. He moved to Surbiton in 1863,
living first at Woodside Cottage in the Ewell Road and later
at Fern Cottage, Dennan Road. He recalled that when he
came to the district, Tolworth consisted of 'a very few and
scattered people, half a dozen cottages, 2 rooms and a few
others here and there, about 30 or 40 people were all that
could be found'. He used to visit the Surrey Militia men
quartered locally, workmen employed in building Christ
Church, employees of the local brickfields and patients at the
Cottage Hospital. At first he preached at an open-air mission
in Cleaveland Road, but later in a mission room built in a
nearby garden. His wife died, aged 70, in 1893. He retired in
1895 through ill health and died, aged 80, in 1904.

99. St Raphael's Roman Catholic church, *c.*1900, which was built by Alexander Raphael on his estate, Surbiton Place. Completed in 1848, it is said to have been the fulfilment of a promise he made to the Virgin Mary for interceding for his recovery from a serious illness.

100. On 26 June 1895 the town was decorated in grand style to welcome the Prince and Princess of Wales who were attending the wedding at St Raphael's of the Duc d'Aosta and the Princess Hélène d'Orléans, great granddaughter of King Louis Philippe of France.

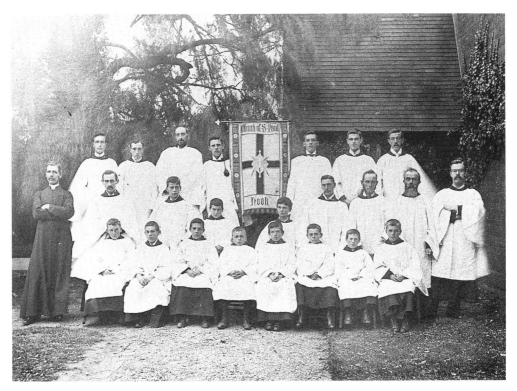

101. The choir of St Paul's, Hook, outside the church porch with the Rev. Charles Edward Block, around the turn of this century. The original parish church of Hook, which stood to the south of the present one, was built in 1838. The existing church dates from 1883.

102. The parish church of St John the Baptist, Old Malden, seen across fields early this century.

Health and Welfare

During the Middle Ages the Church was the chief dispenser of poor relief, aided by the almsgiving of pious laymen and religious and craft guilds, but much of this changed after the Reformation and the dissolution of the monasteries in the 16th century.

The responsibility for the poor and the infirm from the 16th century fell to the parish under the direction of the Justices of the Peace, and it was the duty of the parish overseer to levy a poor rate to provide money for poor families in distress. In addition, local benefactors bequeathed property or money for necessary provisions and education. Amongst Kingston's benefactors was Cecily Hussie, a widow, who died in 1511 bequeathing 13 shirts and smocks to 13 poor men and women, and a mattress, a pair of sheets and an 'old white coverlet' to the local almshouse. In the next century William Cleave left money for new almshouses for 'six poor men and six poor women of honest life and reputation'. The buildings, erected in 1668, still stand in London Road today.

Under an Act of Parliament of 1723 Kingston set up a workhouse in 1725/26 using, temporarily, a house on the Woodbines Estate (near the site of County Hall). Regulations drawn up at the time were strict: inmates were not allowed provisions at breakfast, dinner or supper until their work had been done, candles were to be out by 9 o'clock, no distilled liquors or tobacco were to be brought into the house, and church services were compulsory on Sundays, Wednesdays and Fridays. Typical meals included beef broth for breakfast, 'peas pottage' for dinner, and bread and butter or cheese for supper. Later the parish workhouse moved to 155/157 London Road, the site of a Norbiton bus garage extension.

By the early part of the 19th century the problem of poor relief had grown too great for the parish to bear, and under the Poor Law Amendment Act of 1834 parishes were united into Unions, each with a Board of Guardians elected by the ratepayers. A Union workhouse in Kingston was completed in 1839 and occupied the site later used by Kingston Hospital.

Kingston suffered from the plague in the 17th century and cholera in the 19th, as the parish burial registers testify, and the Town Council minutes refer to a 'pest house' for infectious diseases pulled down in 1703. In the 19th century people were able to contribute to local medical and savings schemes such as the Kingston Provident Dispensary, founded in 1865, and institutions like the Victoria Hospital in Coombe Lane and Surbiton Cottage Hospital. The local authority, too, became more concerned with public health. A Medical Officer was first appointed in 1866 to deal specifically with a cholera outbreak. A permanent officer was appointed from 1873.

Kingston Hospital was brought into the newly-established National Health Service in 1948.

NOTICE TO THE
POOR of KINGSTON.

It has been determined by the Kingston Association to allow Forty Poor Persons, or Families, resident in Kingston, who may wish to do so, to deposit a part of what they earn during the next 32 Weeks, beginning on Saturday April 27th. 1822, and to receive it back again with addition during the next Winter, in order to procure the Articles for which the deposits may be made, namely, Bread, Flour, and Coals only.

RULES.

1. Where there are not more than Four in Family, the Depositor may deposit 2s. 6d. per Month, which in 32 Weeks will amount to £1. and shall receive back £1. 8s.; or he may deposit One Shilling per Week, in all £1. 12s. and shall receive back £2. 5s.

2. Where there are more than Four in Family, the Depositor may either deposit on the same terms as in Rule 1. or be allowed to deposit more, and to receive back a larger increase as follows :

he may deposit 1s. 6d. per Week, in all - - - £2. 8s. 0d.
and shall receive back - - - - £3. 4s. 0d.
or he may deposit 2s. per Week, in all - - - £3. 4s. 0d.
and shall receive back - - - - £4. 2s. 0d.

3. Any Depositor may at any time draw out the whole that he has deposited, (but not a part of it) and in that case he will receive his own again without addition.

4. The way in which the Deposits, together with the addition, will be given back to the Depositor is by Tickets, which will be as good as Money, to be taken to any Dealer in the three Articles named above, with whom the Depositor may choose to deal.

N. B. Attendance will be given on every Saturday Evening from 7 to 8 o'Clock in the Association Room, during the Summer to receive the Deposits, and during the Winter to deliver out the Tickets, which may be applied for.

5. The Depositor shall not be required to deposit every Week, but may do it on those Saturdays when he finds it most convenient, provided that in every eight Weeks he deposits one fourth of the whole amount that he has agreed to deposit : otherwise he will receive back his deposits without any benefit.

6. During the Winter the Depositor may apply for Tickets on any Saturday Evening, provided that he draws out at no one time above one fourth part of his own deposit, and also provided that he does not draw out altogether more than one half of his deposits during the first half of the Winter : but in Winter as well as in Summer he may draw out all his deposits at once, if he chooses to do so without receiving any benefit.

7. The addition allowed upon the sum deposited may not be drawn out at the option of the Depositor, but he will receive every week during Winter such proportion of that addition as may be due for one week.

N. B. Persons wishing to deposit will apply at the Association Room on any Saturday evening at 7 o'Clock, commencing Saturday April 27th.

8. If the list of 40 Persons is full, when the Poor Person applies, he may be admitted on the recommendation from some Gentleman or Lady who is a Subscriber to promote this Plan.

Signed on behalf of the Committee of the Association.

C. N. PALLMER, *Chairman.*
S. W. GANDY. *Treasurer.*
J. S. HAYCRAFT, *Secretaries.*
T. CHALK,

KINGSTON,
April 19th 1822.

737

J. ATTFIELD, PRINTER, MARKET PLACE. KINGSTON.

103. Notice to the poor of Kingston, 19 April 1822. A Kingston Association for bettering the conditions and morals of the poor was formed on 27 November 1817. The first president was Charles Nicholas Pallmer, resident of Norbiton Place. The main concerns of the Association were to encourage the establishment of a savings bank and medical dispensary, to investigate poor housing conditions, to promote Sunday observance and to encourage the use of machines rather than 'climbing boys' for sweeping chimneys. 'Rewards' were paid to deserving poor people on the Association's anniversary each year.

104.   The Royal Cambridge Asylum for destitute soldiers' widows, 1854. The building which stood in Cambridge Road was erected to designs by Thomas Allom. The foundation stone was laid by Prince Albert on 1 May 1852 and the building was opened in February 1854 as a memorial to the 1st Duke of Cambridge who died on 8 July 1850. The cost was £3,700.

105.   The Old Workhouse in London Road, Kingston, *c*.1837. The original building, dating from the 17th century, was a substantial gentleman's residence belonging, in the late 17th and early 18th centuries, to Edward Belitha, a London businessman and local benefactor. It was occupied in the 18th century by Richard Wooddeson, master of Kingston Grammar School, who taught private scholars there. In 1774 the house was sold to Kingston parish as a workhouse and it was occupied as such until 1839 even after the appointment of a Board of Guardians in 1835. The building was too small to be a Union workhouse and a new one was built on Kingston Hill. The old building was sold to Charles Molloy Westmacott, a sculptor, who rebuilt it and gave it a Gothic façade. Later known as 155/157 London Road, Snappers Castle, the buildings were demolished in 1979 to make way for an extension to Norbiton bus garage.

106. Rules of the Kingston Provident Dispensary, early 20th century. The Dispensary, which had its headquarters in the Apple Market in Kingston, was established in 1865 in order that working people would be able to seek medical advice without being compelled to go to the Union or parish for relief.

RULES
For the Guidance of Provident Members.

————※————

Each Member (whether under 12 years of age or not) to pay 1d. per week.

The payment of Provident Members must be made monthly in advance.

No one will be entitled to the benefits of the institution if in arrears, and each Member to pay a fine of a 1d. for the arrears of every month. If any Member be more than six months in arrear, the name shall be erased from the books.

That no person be admitted a Member who shall not satisfy the Committee of Management and the Medical Officer who will be required to attend him, as to his suitability both as regards health and income.

Provident Members living in Kingston, Norbiton, or Kingston Hill may be admitted, and their payments received at the

BOARD ROOM, APPLE MARKET, KINGSTON,

On Saturday Evenings, from May to September inclusive, from 7.30 till 9; from October to April inclusive, from 7 till 8.30. Or if resident in Surbiton, at

DR. OWEN COLEMAN'S, ADELAIDE ROAD,

On the first and third Monday Evenings in the month, from 7.15 to 8. Bank Holidays excepted.

To save the inconvenience of sending their Subscriptions monthly, the Provident Members are permitted to pay a year or any part of it in advance.

On an application for Medical advice, the sick member must present this card to the Medical Officer of his district as shown below. When a member is too ill to attend at the Surgery, he will be visited at his own house, *providing this card be sent and notice given to the Medical Officer not later than the Morning Surgery Hours.*

The District Medical Officers' Surgery Hours (**SUNDAYS EXCEPTED**) are :—

KINGSTON—Dr. Goodman, Richmond Road, between the hours of 9 and 10 in the morning, and 6 and 7.30 in the evening.

NORBITON—Dr. Finny, "Tamesa," Kingston Hill, between 9 and 10 in the morning, and 7.30 to 8.30 in the evening.

SURBITON—Dr. COLEMAN, Adelaide Road, between 9 and 10 in the morning, and 6 to 7 in the evening.

Mr. Ide, Dentist, Elm Lawn, Eden Street, Kingston, gives **ADVICE ONLY,** free to Provident Members at his house on Tuesday, Thursday and Friday mornings, between the hours of 9.30 and 10.30.

A Married Woman who is a Provident Member may be attended in her confinement by the Resident Medical Officer, provided that she shall, one month previously, have paid the fee of 10s. 6d.

In all applications for medical aid, the members must bring their own bottles and strictly attend to the instructions of the Medical Officer.

SANITARY PRECAUTIONS

DURING THE FLOODS.

1. The floods having extended over the gathering ground of our water supplies, it is absolutely necessary that all water should be boiled and filtered before being used.

2. Persons attacked with diarrhœa should seek Medical advice.

3. As soon as the water subsides, get the water pumped or baled out—open all windows and doors to allow of free ingress of fresh air—take up the flooring of basements to dry the space underneath—spread about quicklime to help the drying process—do not close up the floors till the space beneath is thoroughly dry.

4. Disinfectants will be supplied by the Corporation wherever necessary.

5. Further advice can be obtained by applying at this office.

H. BEALE COLLINS,
Medical Officer of Health,

Health Office,
Clattern House,
November 19th, 1894.

W. Drewett, Printer, Market Place, Kingston.

107. Notice posted by the local Medical Officer of Health giving advice on precautions to be taken during recent floods, 19 November 1894.

108. Matron, housemistress and girls of the Kingston Moral Welfare Association, *c.*1899. The Association was established in Kingston in 1895 for the care of 'fallen' girls. Its successor, the Kingston and District Wel-Care Association, now has premises in Canbury Park Road.

109. The quadrangle of Cleaves' Almshouses in London Road, Kingston, 1953.
William Cleave, by his will dated 1665, left money and property to the
Corporation for the erection of almshouses for the maintenance of 12 poor people
in the parish of Kingston. The buildings, with six 'houses' on each side of a
gabled entrance, were erected in 1668. Additional 'houses' were erected in 1883
for four extra inmates, and two more, for married couples, were funded by
Mrs. Ranyard whose husband was Mayor in 1847.

110. Turning the first sod for the Kingston Victoria Hospital in Coombe Road on 22 June 1897. The hospital
was to be erected in honour of Queen Victoria's Diamond Jubilee. On the day of the Jubilee, an exceptionally hot
one, the Mayoress, Mrs. A. W. Homersham, arrived to perform the ceremony. There was, according to the *Surrey
Comet*, some confusion as to where this should take place. 'All that was to be seen on the field itself were a couple
of men leisurely mowing a pathway through the long grass and a flock of sheep taking a siesta beneath the trees'.
The hospital was opened one year later, on 12 December 1898, by the Duke of Cambridge. Before it was built
accident cases and patients needing surgery were treated either at the Royal Hospital in Richmond or Surbiton
Cottage Hospital. The building subsequently became part of Kingston Hospital. A 'New' Victoria Hospital was
established in a converted house in Coombe Lane in 1954.

111a. & b. (*Above*) The Kingston Infirmary, after 1902, and (*below*) a children's ward in 1920. The Infirmary was originally administered as part of Kingston Union Workhouse by the Board of Guardians. In 1902 new buildings were erected and the institution was given a separate administration. During the First World War a portion of the Infirmary buildings was used for the reception of wounded soldiers. After the war, in 1920, the hospital was renamed the Kingston and District Hospital to remove prejudices felt by many who still considered it a workhouse institution.

112. The opening of the nurses' home at the Kingston and District Hospital in 1928. Plans for the expansion of the hospital were prepared in 1924-25 by F. Danby Smith. These included a new porters' lodge, offices, casualty department, more wards and a nurses' home. The home was to be four storeys high to accommodate 100 nurses, five sisters and four assistant matrons. The foundation stone of the home was laid in 1927 and it was opened on 29 March 1928 by the Duke and Duchess of York (later King George VI and Queen Elizabeth).

113. Aerial view of the Kingston and District Hospital photographed when the nurses' home was opened in 1928. The imposing building (top right), where Blenheim Gardens now stand, is the Princess Louise Home erected from the designs of H. Saxon Snell. It was purchased from the Metropolitan Convalescent Institution by the National Society for the Protection of Young Girls, and opened by Princess Louise, Marchioness of Lorne, on 20 April 1892. The institution later became the Dalziel-Wooller Memorial Home and was presented in 1933 to Dr. Barnardo's by Lady Dalziel in memory of her husband.

Wartime

A War Office order in 1899 for the mobilisation of reservists had the effect of calling many men in Kingston and neighbourhood suddenly away from home and family to fight in the Boer War. The *Surrey Comet* reported that 'Kingstonians rose to the occasion and gave the troops a fitting send off', as the first contingent left the barracks of the East Surrey Regiment in Kings Road on the way to Surbiton Station. There the men were handed several hundred packets of tobacco by Messrs. Townly & Co. of Surbiton, and 'two young ladies were observed distributing cigarettes'. All subsequent departures were witnessed by 'gigantic crowds' and when peace was proclaimed in May 1902 there were 'scenes of wild rejoicing: all Kingston seemed to be abroad ... the Market Place was well nigh impassable'. Kingston's station master, Mr. Mansell, determined that his own station should have the honour of welcoming the 3rd (Militia) Battalion of the East Surrey Regiment home at the end of June 1902, made secret arrangements that they should alight there rather than at Surbiton.

During the war the people of Kingston organised concerts in aid of the troops and contributed generously to appeals for funds for the families left behind, including the Soldiers and Sailors' Families' Association of which the Princess of Wales (later Queen Alexandra) was president. In December 1899 the Town Council opened an equipment fund to provide the men at the front with necessities. The Mayor is reported as saying that Kingston should set an example, since the battalion had no regimental transport weapons and did not possess a machine gun. Most remarkable of all was the contribution made by Mr. Alfred Cooper of the Gables, Surbiton, now Hillcroft College, who converted his private theatre into a hospital for wounded soldiers.

Recruitment for the First World War received the same enthusiastic response. 'Flocking to the Colours, Splendid Response to Lord Kitchener's Appeal, Enthusiastic Scenes throughout the District, Kingston District Leading' were the headlines in the *Surrey Comet* in September 1914. Large numbers of recruits were brought into Kingston Barracks by motor cars lent by residents. Most of the cars carried patriotic flags and some arrived loaded with men inside and out.

At the end of the first year of hostilities funds for the relief of distress had been established, a subscription had been raised for a Kingston and District Ambulance for the front, and the Board of Guardians' farm premises in Kingston Road, New Malden, had been turned into a Kingston and District Red Cross Hospital (now the Morris Markowe Unit). Training was arranged for local V.A.D.s and the Third Home Counties' Field Ambulance R.A.M.C. established its base in Claremont Road, Surbiton. Children also contributed to the war effort. Boys from the public elementary schools in the Borough made bedside lockers for the hospital and pupils of Tiffin Girls' School made curtains.

By the end of 1915, 14,387 men had enlisted at Kingston Barracks. In Hook, it was said 'every male resident of military age had joined some branch or other of his Majesty's forces'. But the clouds were darkening as more and more names of missing or dead appeared in the columns of the newpapers, and at the end of the war the records of the fallen collected by Kingston Borough Council for the roll of honour tell of sad stories of sacrifice and bravery.

During the Second World War, Kingston, Surbiton, and Malden and Coombe were all units of Group 9 of the London Civil Defence Region. Group headquarters were based at County Hall. Recruitment and training of air-raid precautions and civil defence volunteers began as early as 1937 and continued throughout the war. Malden and Coombe was the first to put the emergency services to the test when, on 16 August 1940, 150 bombs were dropped on the Borough, damaging 1,300 homes and severely disrupting water and transport services. A high proportion of the 552 casualties which Malden suffered throughout the war were caused by that raid.

Kingston claimed the distinction of being the first authority in the country to put its fire guard plan into operation following a mammoth exercise in July 1943, and it was revealed after the war (1945) that frogmen had been trained secretly for confidential war work at the Coronation Swimming Baths in Denmark Road.

As in the First World War, the H. G. Hawker Engineering Company (earlier called the Sopwith Aviation Company) based at Kingston played a crucial part in wartime aircraft production. The Leyland works in Richmond Road (leased from the Aircraft Company in 1928) were converted to military vehicle and munitions production, landing craft for the Normandy and North African landings were made by the building firm, Gazes', and Perrings Department Store (then in Fife Road) turned over the upper floors of its building to the production of armature coils for radio sets. The American forces had their base in nearby Bushey Park and Eisenhower had his country retreat at Telegraph Cottage on Kingston Hill.

After the war, in 1945, Kingston was 'adopted' by Wakefield, West Yorkshire, and received gifts of furniture and household utensils to replace much that was lost in wartime bombing raids.

114a.   Private hospital for wounded soldiers in Surbiton, 1900. Wounded soldiers returning from South Africa on the *Princess of Wales* hospital ship received every kind of comfort and care at a small private hospital at the Gables, Surbiton, owned by Alfred Cooper, a tea merchant. At his own expense, Mr. Cooper converted and equipped a private theatre which had been built in the grounds of his house. The auditorium and stage became 'wards', the star dressing room was equipped as a matron's room and the cloakroom was converted to a doctor's surgery. The Nurses' Association in Claremont Road provided assistance and local bakers supplied bread. For his efforts Mr. Cooper received a knighthood in 1901. The Gables is now Hillcroft College for Women. The theatre has not survived.

114b. A medal commemorating Surbiton's private military hospital.

115. The Mayor, Alderman Salmon, welcoming home the Volunteer Service Company from South Africa in 1901. The people of Kingston and Surbiton staged an enthusiastic reception for the Company's homecoming in June 1901. Flags decorated the shops *en route* from Surbiton Station, and streamers and bunting were suspended from the Town Hall in the Market Place, the balcony of which was reserved for ladies. As the volunteers passed the *Kingston Hotel* on their way to the Barracks they gave a hearty cheer for the proprietor, Mr. W. Munday, in recognition of his kindness in sending them weekly parcels of illustrated newspapers.

116.   Mass recruitment meeting at New Malden on 5 September 1914. A stirring appeal was made to the young men of Malden by Mr. James W. Johnson, clerk of the Maldens and Coombe Urban District Council, who was also the honorary secretary of the Local Emergency and Recruiting Committees. The object of the rally, held at Beverley Park, was to recruit 200 men to form two companies of the 7th (Service) Battalion of the East Surrey Regiment then being formed in Kingston. The idea was that local men should all serve together. The meeting was attended by 2,000 people and 30 men were mustered as volunteers.

COMFORTS FOR THE TROOPS.

HAVING recently executed large Contracts for the Troops, and many other orders at present on hand, enable us to offer these goods at exceptional prices. Early application should be made for them - to secure at present prices.

Blankets, having purchased largely before the war crisis, we are able to offer at old contract prices, in Brown and Grey, as supplied for Army contracts **3/6, 4/9, 6/3 each.**

Fancy Blankets limited quantity only **2/11½, 3/5½, 4/11**

Flannels, Grey, Red, and other colours, for garments for the wounded **10¾d, 1/0¾, 1/3¾, 1/6¾ per yd.**

Warm Flannelettes in all colours ... **3¾d., 4¾d., 6¼d., 8¼d. per yd.**

Woollen Cap Comforters, a necessity for active service, a real soldier's comfort ... ... **1/0¾ each.**

Flannel Shirts, Superior quality, similar to the thousands we have supplied for Army contracts ... **4/11 each.**

Marching Socks in heather mixtures or grey, heavily ribbed, approved pattern **10½d. per pair**

Woollen Jackets, black or dark brown, the soldier's greatest necessity **4/11 each**

Shetland Pants, natural grey shades, warm & comfortable **2/6 & 2/11**

Mittens, Woollen, warm and cosy... **8½d. per pair**

Woollen Vests, natural colour ... **2/6 & 2/11**

Comfortable Slippers for the wounded, felt or leather soles **1/11½ each**

Nurses Ward Shoes with rubber heels... ... ... **1/10½ per pair**

Warm Woollen Gloves in heather mixtures, as supplied for Army **1/-, 1/3 & 1/6 per pair**

ARMY KIT ACCESSORIES.

Army Kit Bags ... ... **3/- each.**

Strong Elastic Web Braces, good leather fittings, as suppled to troops **10d. per pair**

Military Hair Brushes, good bristles, ebonized or satinwood frames ... **1/3 each**

Regulation Shaving Brushes ... **4/6 doz.**

Regulation Tooth Brushes... ... **3/9 doz.**

Hair Combs, strong ... ... **4/6 doz.**

Nickle Forks (army pattern) ... **4/6 doz.**

Table Knives (army pattern) ... **4/6 doz.**

Nickle Table Spoons (army pattern) **4/6 doz.**

Army Towels (Turkish) ... ... **9½d. each.**

Army Razors ... ... **1/- each.**

Regulation Army Holdalls, to hold brushes, soap, comb, razors, and other accessories, well made ... **6½d. each.**

Hussifs, as approved by Army authorities, well filled with needles, thread, buttons, thimble, and everything necessary for repairs ... ... **6½d. each.**

OVER SIXTY DEPARTMENTS.

Bentalls

KINGSTON-ON-THAMES.

'Phone : ONE Kingston.

117. 'Comforts for the troops', advertised for sale by Bentall's Department Store in October 1914. Appeals for money to purchase 'comforts' to send to France were a feature of numerous First World War fund raising efforts. In addition, badly needed hospital clothing and medical supplies were made by 'lady war workers' at the Surbiton and neighbourhood War Hospital Supply Depot at Croft House, 74 Ewell Road, which was opened in October 1915.

118a. & b. Kingston held a lavish war market and pageant in the Market Place on 19 June 1917 to raise money for the East Surrey Regiment Comforts Fund and other war charities. Items for auction included Queen Victoria's market basket, pin cushions made from a dress of Queen Alexandra's (donated by Queen Mary), and rifles which Lord Kitchener had captured in East Africa. Many actors and actresses helped on the stalls or gave afternoon theatrical performances, among them Gerald Du Maurier and George Robey, and thousands of spectators watched the Elizabethan pageant organised by the novelist Miss Winifred Graham (Mrs. Theodore Cory). The event raised £4,400.

Kingston Great War Market

To be Held on TUESDAY, 19th JUNE, 1917.

Organiser: **Mrs. CORY** ("WINIFRED GRAHAM").

Hon. Treasurer:	Hon. Secretaries:
THE MAYOR OF KINGSTON. (ALDERMAN C. H. BURGE).	MR. ROBERT G. GRAHAM, MR. THEODORE CORY, Old Place, Hampton Court, Middx. Telephone: 763 KINGSTON.

Under the Distinguished Patronage of
HIS WORSHIP THE MAYOR AND MAYORESS OF KINGSTON.

EVELYN DUCHESS OF WELLINGTON
THE MARQUESS AND MARCHIONESS OF RIPON
CONSTANCE COUNTESS DE LA WARR
THE LADY MARION WELLER
THE LADY EMMA TALBOT
THE LADY MARY GRIFFIN
THE LADY MARGARET SACKVILLE
THE LADY ROSSMORE
THE LADY HILLINGDON
THE LADY GERALDINE ST. LAWRENCE
THE LADY HENRIETTA GUINNESS

THE RT. HON. LORD & LADY ASHCOMBE
THE RT. HON. LORD ROTHERHAM
THE RT. HON. LORD AND LADY TENTERDEN
THE LADY GEORGIANA PEEL
THE RT. HON. SIR GEORGE AND LADY CAVE
THE LADY AUGUSTUS HERVEY
VIOLET LADY GREVILLE
THE LADY SWAYTHLING
SIR WALTER AND LADY TREVELYAN
LADY SINCLAIR OF DUNBEATH
LADY HART

SIR FRANK AND LADY NEWNES
SIR CLIFFORD CORY, BART., M.P.
GENERAL SIR BINDON AND LADY BLOOD
SIR THOMAS AND LADY SUTHERLAND
GENERAL SIR ALFRED AND LADY TURNER
SIR MONTAGUE AND LADY OMMANNEY
LADY MACGREGOR
LADY MARK
LADY DE RUTZEN
LADY DE GEX
LADY VOGEL

HELP !   HELP !!   HELP !!!

Send **everything** and **anything** to be Sold at the many fascinating Stalls.
Send Money.   Get everyone you know to **Come and Buy.**

LOOK WHAT IT IS FOR.   Then you MUST respond to this appeal.

EAST SURREY REGIMENT COMFORTS AND PRISONERS OF WAR; KINGSTON, SURBITON AND DISTRICT RED CROSS HOSPITAL; LOCAL WAR HOSPITAL SUPPLY DEPOTS, AFFILIATED TO QUEEN MARY'S NEEDLEWORK GUILD, CAVENDISH SQUARE.

A GRAND PAGEANT
Under the direction of Dr. W. E. St. L. FINNY, J.P.

THE MARCHIONESS TOWNSHEND as "QUEEN ELIZABETH," with her Court and Followers.   A Magnificent and Imposing Spectacle.

THEATRICAL PERFORMANCES

In the TOWN HALL by EMINENT LONDON ARTISTS.

ELIZABETHAN PAGEANT
KINGSTON ON THAMES
JUNE 19/17

119.   First World War work at the Sopwith Aviation Company. Many women were employed by the company during the war. They are seen in this photograph applying special camouflage to a TF2 Salamander.

120.   A Mark V horse-drawn ambulance wagon, possibly of the 3rd/3rd Home Counties Field Ambulance, Royal Army Medical Corps on field exercises at New Malden, during the First World War, 1915/16. During the war a motor ambulance for the front, a 15 h.p. Crossley car, fitted with a covering bearing the red cross on the sides and bonnet so that it could also be seen from an aeroplane, was purchased from subscriptions raised by readers of the *Surrey Comet*.

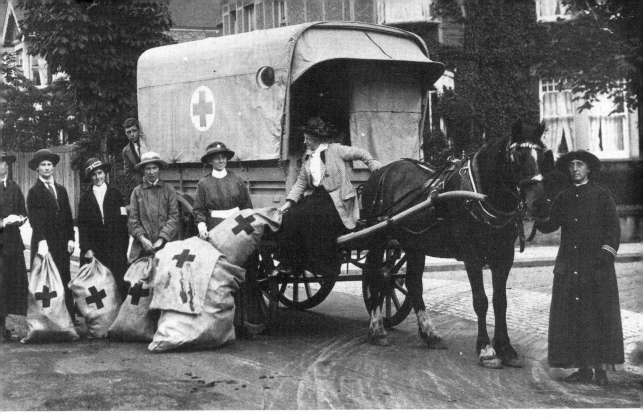

121. Waste paper collection during the First World War: £287 was collected by the Urban District of Malden and Coombe.

122. The 9th (Service) Battalion, East Surrey Regiment, in Kingston Market Place on 20 November 1919. The Battalion, raised in September 1914, embarked at Folkestone for France on 31 August 1915 and served in many of the famous engagements of the war including Loos, Passchendaele and Cambrai. After the war they formed part of the British Army of occupation on the Rhine and, after disbandment, returned to England in November 1919. On 20 November 1919 Col. E. A. Cameron, Major J. C. Brown, six other officers and 54 other ranks, proceeded to Kingston where the Mayoress placed a laurel wreath on the colour. The party was afterwards entertained to lunch by the Mayor and Corporation.

123. 'Welcome Home' scene at Malden and Coombe, 28 August 1920. This was planned to be more lavish than the peace celebrations. A civic procession preceded a reception at Beverley Park where ex-servicemen were presented with illuminated certificates.

124.   Demonstration air-raid trench just inside the south entrance to King Edward Recreation Ground, Hook, 1938.

125.   An air-raid warden's post on the Portsmouth Road at Surbiton, in use during the Second World War.

126a. & b.   Bomb damage in Surbiton and New Malden, 1940. The church of St Mark, Surbiton, was almost totally destroyed by a fire bomb which fell on 2 October 1940. The photograph above is taken from the remains of the west door. Fourteen days later, on 16 October, the Borough Council offices of Malden and Coombe were damaged, but fortunately not completely destroyed. The photograph below shows the clearing up operation in progress.

127.   Salvage of waste paper in Surbiton in 1941.

128a. & b.   The construction of landing barges on the premises of W. H. Gaze & Son, builders, of High Street, Kingston, in 1943. Following construction they were taken to the river for launching.

"WINGS FOR VICTORY"

IN THE ROYAL BOROUGH OF

KINGSTON
-UPON-THAMES

MAY 22nd — MAY 29th

OPENING CEREMONY MAY 22nd AT 12 NOON, OUTSIDE GUILDHALL, by AIR MARSHAL SIR TRAFFORD LEIGH-MALLORY, K.C.B., D.S.O., Air Officer Commanding in Chief, Fighter Command, R.A.F. Supported by CAPTAIN A. MARTINI, Pilot of "THE DRY MARTINI" BOMBER, American Air Force, ADMIRAL SIR PERCY ROYDS, C.B., C.M.G., M.P. His Worship The Mayor, SIR EDWARD SCARLES, O.B.E., J.P., Members of Corporation and guests.

Procession and march past of Service units, Civil Defence, and local organisations; Sir Trafford Leigh-Mallory taking the salute at Guildhall, at 3 p.m.

For fuller detail of the above and following summary of the week's events see official programme

11 a.m. SUNDAY. Civic attendance at Parish Church followed by March Past of Units attending. H.W. the Mayor will take the Salute in front of Guildhall.	**12 noon. THURSDAY.** Flying Officer Redmond, Pilot in the Battle for Britain, will speak from Guildhall.	WARDENS, HOUSEWIVES AND FIREGUARD EVENTS. FULL DETAILS IN PROGRAMME, OR FROM WARDEN'S POST AS NUMBER IN SIDE COLUMN.

DAILY EVENTS

3 p.m. American Baseball Match at Leylands' Sports Ground.
6.30 p.m. Grand Celebrity Concert at the Empire (under direction of Gerald Santall, Esq.).
11.30 a.m. MONDAY (Empire Day). Children's Rally at Guildhall. Royal Canadian Air Force Band.

2.30 p.m. Bridge Drive at Guildhall.
3 p.m. Gramophone Recital—Maxwell's, Clarence Street.
6 p.m. Mixed Bowls Tournament — Canbury Gardens.
7.30 p.m. American Air Force Orchestra (Flying Yanks) and Open Air Dance—Canbury Gardens.
9.30 p.m.

12 noon. TUESDAY. The Rev. Wellesley Orr, M.A., M.B.E., will speak from Guildhall.
3 p.m. Gramophone Recital, Maxwell's, Clarence Street.
5 to 7 p.m. Market and Games. British Restaurant.
7 p.m. Film Exhibition, Tiffin School.
7.30 p.m. Dance at Claremont Hall.
8 p.m. A.T.C. Band, Queen's Promenade.

12 noon. FRIDAY. Admiral Sir Percy Royds, C.B., C.M.G., M.P., will speak from Guildhall.
3 p.m. Gramophone Recital, Maxwell's, Clarence Street.
7 p.m. N.F.S. Drill Display—Canbury Gardens.

2.30 p.m. WEDNESDAY. Whist Drive and Tea at Guildhall.
3 p.m. Cricket Match—Grammar School Ground.
7.30 p.m. Warden's Variety Entertainment at Tiffin Boys' School.
7.30 p.m. East Surrey Regimental Band—Canbury Gardens.

11.30 a.m. SATURDAY. A.T.C. Band, Guildhall.
12 noon. H.W. the Mayor will speak from Guildhall.
8 p.m. Miss Lena Taylor's Concert, with K.A.D.O.S. —St. John's Hall, Grove Lane.

ELEPHANTS WILL TOUR THE TOWN THIS DAY.

	Post
DAILY Old World Bring and Buy Fair, Guildhall	12
,, Bring and Buy Sale	1
,, Fun Fair, Elm Road Recreation Ground	7
MAY 22 Dance, St. John's Hall, Grove Lane	14
,, 25 Whist Drive, Willoughby Arms	6
to Procession — Sea Scouts, Decorated Cycles, Fancy Costumes, Bank Lane	8
25 Whist Drive, Scouts Hall, Park Road	3
Auction Sale	5
,, 26 Dance, Claremont Hall	10
Fun Fair, Shirley Hall, Alexandra Road	4
Scout Rally and Comic Cricket Match, Kingstonians Ground	8
,, 27 Whist Drive, St. John's Hall, Grove Lane	4
Bring and Buy Sale and Exhibition, Competitions, Scouts' Hall, Park Road	3
Fun Fair, Shirley Hall, Alexandra Road	4
,, 28 "Wings for Victory" Sale, Latchmere Road School	2
Bring and Buy Sale and Exhibition, Competitions, Scouts' Hall, Park Road	3
Dance, Zeeta Cafe	9
Whist Drive, 15, Portsmouth Road	15
Dance, Grove Tavern, Washington Road	12

DAILY EVENTS

AT GUILDHALL
HAWKER-HURRI BOMBER
'PLANE WING AND MACHINE GUN

AT BENTALLS'
AERIAL WAR AND BOMB EXHIBITION
AND
MERLIN AERO ENGINE

AT GAS COMPANY
SHOW ROOMS—THAMES STREET
PHOTOGRAPHS OF KINGSTONIANS
IN R.A.F.
EXHIBITS OF POSTERS COMPETITION

AT WAR SAVINGS CENTRE
19 CLARENCE STREET
DISPLAY OF MODEL AIRCRAFT
(IN WINDOWS)

TARGET — £500,000 (100 TYPHOONS)

Everyone in the Borough it is expected will do their utmost to invest to the limit during the week, to secure a record result representative of their regard and admiration for the gallant men of the Air Force which is doing so much towards winning the war. SEND YOUR SAVINGS SKY HIGH

129. Programme for Kingston's 'Wings for Victory' week, 22-29 May 1943. By the last evening of the week the target of £500,000 had been topped by £70,000 and a new target of £800,000 was set. One of the features of the week was a grand egg auction held during a wardens' variety performance at Tiffin Boys' School. The bidding for a dozen eggs started at 5s. and closed at £3 15s. Two elephants from Chessington Zoo also contributed to the Wings Week by parading through the streets to encourage donations.

Leisure, Sports and Special Events

Morris dancing, annual May Day games and colourful Robin Hood dramas enacted at All Saints' church were features of life in Kingston in the 16th and 17th centuries as were the three annual fairs held by right of the royal charters at Whitsun, July/August and in the autumn. Townspeople gathered regularly (or hid behind closed doors) and children played truant from school, when the traditional football match was played in the Market Place on Shrove Tuesday. Eighteenth-century Town Council minutes record payments for entrance to a bowling green to the south of the Market Place, and a lease of land in 1565 allowed access for archers to shoot at a 'round' (close to the present County Hall site). Gaming tables and skittle alleys were often associated with local public houses – there was a skittle alley at the *Sun Hotel* in the Market Place (later Woolworths) – and magistrates were often forced to issue instructions for the orderly conduct of alehouses and Sunday observance.

The River Thames, now predominantly used for pleasure, was originally a main trading route. Alderman Gould, reminiscing about his early days in Kingston, remarked that in the late 1830s 'going out on a boat for pleasure was never heard of'. This soon changed. The Kingston Rowing Club was founded in 1858 and an annual regatta became 'one of the most important of the many social summer gatherings of fashionable Surbiton' – the rendezvous was Raven's Ait.

Swimming, cycling, football, cricket, hockey, tennis, and golf were sports well represented in the area. For the less energetic a stroll in nearby Richmond Park or one of the local recreation grounds, Canbury Gardens, for example, or attending one of the many annual events, Surbiton Horse Show, a flower show in Malden, or a 'bicycle gymkhana' (like the one held at Surbiton Lawn Tennis Club in 1899), may have been more to their taste.

A glance through past numbers of the *Surrey Comet* indicates how many local societies of all kinds Kingston and district supported, catering for all interests, among them a Debating Society founded in 1886, a Photographic Society founded in 1893 (considered in 1899 to be the largest of its kind in England) and a Kingston and Surbiton Chrysanthemum Society which in 1899 had already held 23 annual exhibitions.

Kingston was well provided with theatres and cinemas. Surbiton Assembly Rooms opened in 1889 and is still used for dances, meetings and theatrical events. The Royal County Theatre in Fife Road survived from 1897 to 1912 as a theatre, and until 1940 as a cinema, Kingston Empire in Richmond Road was a music hall between 1910 and 1955, and the Elite Cinema on the present C & A site showed films between 1921 and 1955.

Last but not least were the lavish pageants like the Three Towns' Pageant of 1951 (organised by Kingston, Richmond and Twickenham at Hampton Court as part of the Festival of Britain), and other festivities organised so enthusiastically by local people to celebrate important historic events, royal coronations and anniversaries, and captured so aptly by the cameraman for future generations to enjoy.

TOWN

OF

Kingston-upon-Thames,

SURREY.

IT IS ORDERED BY THE MAGISTRATES,

That all Ale-house Keepers within this Town and the Liberty thereof, do shut up their Houses at *Eleven* o'Clock in the Evening, and not open the same before *Six* o'Clock in the Morning in Summer, and *Seven* in the Winter; and also keep their Houses close shut (except to Travellers) and not suffer any Person to remain Drinking therein during the time of Divine Service on Sundays, Christmas Day, and Good Friday.

They are also strictly commanded, not to harbour any Apprentice, nor suffer any Person to continue Tippling, nor any Gaming, or profane Cursing or Swearing; nor to serve any Liquor to Persons appearing to be in a State of apparent Intoxication; or who receive Parochial Relief; nor harbour Prostitutes, reputed Thieves, Rogues, Vagabonds, or other idle or disorderly Persons; nor permit any Seditious, or other unlawful Clubs or Combinations, Entertainments of the Stage, Public Music or Dancing, Bull, Bear or Badger Baiting, Cock Fighting or Boxing; nor permit Seditious or indecent Publications or Prints to be exposed; nor any Soldiers to run up Scores upon the Credit of their Accoutrements; or any Pay Table to be open later than Nine o'Clock in the Evening.

It is also Ordered that all Shopkeepers within the said Town and Liberty, do keep their Shops close shut, after Nine o'Clock in the Morning on Sundays, Christmas Day, and Good Friday; and that they do not sell or expose to sale after that Hour, on either of the said Days, in their Shops or elsewhere, any Goods or Wares whatsoever.

And all Persons are strictly forbid playing at Foot Ball, Cricket or any other Game whatsoever on Sundays, in any open or inclosed Field or Highway within the Jurisdiction aforesaid.

And all Constables, Headboroughs, and other Officers are charged and commanded to be particularly attentive to their Duty in enforcing the execution of the Laws relating to the above Particulars: And to give Information of all Persons who shall be found offending against the same.

Jemmett,

Town Clerk.

W. STRANGE, PRINTER.

130.   Order issued early in the 19th century by the magistrates of Kingston for the orderly conduct of ale houses and Sunday observance.

131. Football at Kingston on Shrove Tuesday, c.1860. Football festivals were traditionally held in Kingston on Shrove Tuesday but caused a great deal of disturbance in the neighbourhood. In 1840, the Borough Council complained that the game was 'an obstruction to the passengers, a great annoyance to the peaceable inhabitants, subversive of good order and prejudicial to the morality of the town', and asked for Metropolitan Police protection. The Borough Council considered banning the game in 1859 but the provision of a 'people's park' was suggested as a solution. This was never put into practice and the continuing popularity of the game during the 19th century can perhaps be measured by the number of children who went absent from school to be present on the occasion.

132. 'Welcome Home' to the Kingstonian Football Club by the Mayor, Sir Alfred Woodgate, after winning the F.A. Amateur Cup in 1933. The club, an amalgamation of Kingston A.F.C. and Old Kingstonians, was founded in 1885.

133. Poster advertising the facilities of the Corporation Baths in Wood Street, 1898. These baths, opened in 1897, replaced the floating bath on the Thames (*see* plate 137). In 1936/7 new 'Coronation Baths' were constructed in Denmark Road, but were replaced in 1983 by the present Kingfisher Baths next to Kingston Library.

Borough of Kingston-upon-Thames.

CORPORATION

PUBLIC BATHS
WOOD STREET
(Three minutes walk from Kingston, L. & S.W.R. Station; one minute from Thames Side).

These Baths are OPEN TO THE PUBLIC DAILY, and Tickets are issued and stamped up to half-an-hour of the time of closing as follows, viz:—

THE SWIMMING BATH

MONDAYS & FRIDAYS:
GENTLEMEN from 6.30 a.m. to 9 a.m., and from 2.30 p.m. to 9 p.m. ... ... } **6d.**
LADIES from 9.30 a.m. to 2 p.m. ... ...

WEDNESDAYS:
GENTLEMEN from 6.30 a.m. to 9 a.m., and from 5.30 p.m. to 9 p.m. ... ... } **6d.**
LADIES from 9.30 a.m. to 5 p.m. ... ...

TUESDAYS & THURSDAYS:
GENTLEMEN from 6.30 a.m. to 11.30 a.m., and from 4.30 p.m. to 9 p.m. ... ... } **2d.**
LADIES from 12 noon to 4 p.m.... ... ...

SATURDAYS:
GENTLEMEN from 6.30 a.m. to 9 p.m. ... ... **2d.**

SUNDAY MORNINGS:
GENTLEMEN from 6.30 a.m. to 9 a.m. ... ... **2d.**

The above Charge of 6d. includes Two Towels and Bathing Dress.
In addition to the above Charge of 2d., a Penny extra to be charged for One Towel and Bathing Dress.
LIBERAL ARRANGEMENTS FOR CLUBS, SCHOOLS, &c.
Experienced Swimming Instructors for Ladies and Gentlemen are in attendance daily. All Swimming Lessons by appointment.

··

THE SLIPPER BATHS

Are open to Ladies and Gentlemen from 6.30 a.m. to 9 p.m. on Week-Days at the following Charges :—

First Class Warm Bath (Two Towels) ... ... **6d.**
First Class Cold Bath (Two Towels) ... ... **3d.**
Second Class Warm Bath (One Towel) ... ... **3d.**
Second Class Cold Bath (One Towel)... ... ... **1d.**
SOAP ONE PENNY EXTRA.

Any further information can be obtained of Mr. Gerald O'Rourke, Superintendent, The Baths, Wood Street, Kingston-upon-Thames.

1st March, 1898. By order of the Baths Committee. HAROLD A. WINSER, Town Clerk.

W. Drewett & Sons, Printers, Market Place, Kingston.

134. The Surbiton Lagoon in 1960. The popular Surbiton Lagoon was opened in 1934 but was finally closed in 1980. Freak floods on 7 August 1960 caused considerable damage in the area and forced the temporary closure of the pool. A notice stating 'closed no water' belies the real situation on that day. In contrast, attendance in August 1945, because of exceptionally fine weather, reached a peak of 3,600.

135. The Annual Surrey Lawn Tennis Championships at Surbiton in 1907, at which Mrs. A. Sterry (formerly Miss Charlotte Cooper), five times Wimbledon champion, beat Mrs. Lambert-Chambers in the final of the Ladies' Open Singles. The Surbiton Lawn Tennis and Squash Rackets Club, originally called the Berrylands Club, was founded in 1881 and took over the members of the Surbiton Cricket Club whose grounds were on the opposite side of the road. At the outset there were 200 members, 11 grass courts and a croquet lawn. In 1899 the committee decided to promote a Lawn Tennis Tournament for Surrey players and from 1904 a full Open Tournament was held annually. Mrs. Helen Wills Moody and Maureen 'Little Mo' Connolly were among the many famous players who have taken part in the championships. The first squash court was built in 1936 and others followed.

136. A Kingston Congregational church tennis party in 1913 at Southernhay, Hook Road, the home of Mr. and Mrs. Thompson. The Rev. J. C. Harris is in the back row.

137.   Two cyclists with an 'ordinary' bicycle, now popularly known as the 'penny farthing', being photographed beside the Thames in the 1880s. On the opposite side of the river, on the Kingston side, is the town's first swimming bath, which was opened in July 1880. Designed by the famous engineer, John Dixon, who lived in the Portsmouth Road, the pool was a floating platform on the river, 100 feet long by 27 feet wide. 'There is every reason to hope', the *Surrey Comet* commented, 'that the venture will promote habits of cleanliness in the lower orders'. The platform remained in position for 12 years in spite of violent disputes between the council and the Thames Conservators about its positioning.

138.   The Surrey Athletic Club Marathon Race at New Malden in 1909. This event, which took place on Boxing Day, was the second annual 'marathon' to be sponsored by the Surrey Athletic Club. The course, which began at the *Royal Oak* and ended at the *Railway Hotel* near New Malden Station, was 23 miles long. Of the 45 competitors, 24 completed the course. The winner was E. Sims of the Uxbridge Athletic Club, who covered the distance in 2 hours, 22 minutes and 13 seconds.

139. Regatta at Raven's Ait, *c.*1900. The Kingston Rowing Club was formed in 1858 and established its headquarters at Raven's Ait from where it held annual regattas. In 1890 the Mayor, Councillor James East, proposed the establishment of a regatta in which all the rowing clubs of the town could take part. The first 'Borough of Kingston Regatta' was held in July that year. Princess Frederica of Hanover, the Duke and Duchess of Teck, the Duke of Cambridge and Baron Von Pawel Rammingen became patrons.

140.   The opening of Canbury Gardens on 3 November 1890. The new 'promenade' along the river adjoining the sewage works had been in constant use by the public for six months before a decision was made to hold a formal opening. Alderman Gould, who was on the sub-committee which laid out the gardens, announced that the approach across Cook's Meadow had been made with 6,000 cubic yards of earth from tunnelling works which were being undertaken by the water company. About 2,600 trees and shrubs were planted and around 7,000 yards of turf laid. Further extensions to the gardens followed.

141.   A view of Queen's Promenade and the river, near St Raphael's church, c.1900.

142.   Presentation by Councillor Belcher of a fountain for Queen's Promenade. The Promenade had been constructed in the 1850s, along the river to the south of the town, from earth excavated by the Chelsea Water Works for their reservoir in the Portsmouth Road. It was extended later in the century. William Belcher was a Kingston Councillor from 1898 to 1900. During his term of office he also suggested that the Town Hall, which he described as inadequate and a discredit to the town, should be rebuilt, and offered to donate the bricks. His offer was rejected.

143. A drink at the *Wagon and Horses* public house in Surbiton Road, *c*.1900.

One Visit—means Many

KINGSTON EMPIRE

Proprietors : The Kingshot Theatres Ltd.
Theatrical Director, Secretary & Licensee : STANLEY WATSON

6.30 TWICE NIGHTLY 8.50

Telephones : KINGSTON 3131 (4 Lines)
BOX OFFICE OPEN 10 a.m. to 10 p.m.

•

*Visited only by the Best Revues,
Musical Comedies and Variety Artistes*

144. The foyer of the Kingston Empire pictured in an advertisement of *c*.1937.

145a. & b. Two July flower shows: (*above*) in Malden and Coombe in 1908 and (*below*) at St Peter's School, Norbiton, *c*.1920.

146. Celebrations at New Malden on Friday 23 June 1911 for the coronation of King George V and Queen Mary. The first event of the day was the unveiling of a public clock presented to New Malden by a local anonymous donor. A procession to Beverley Park followed, led by the 3rd Battalion East Surrey Regiment, and the Day and Sunday School children. On the Thursday, the actual day of the coronation, a huge bonfire was organised.

CORONATION CELEBRATION
NEW MALDEN JUNE 23/11

149.   Esther Hammerton, Kingston's famous sextoness (1711-46), pictured here with her hand on a skull and carrying a sickle, both symbols of life's transience. She is wearing a male waistcoat and hat. Her father had been sexton at All Saints' church but was killed in 1730 when the remains of Kingston's Saxon chapel collapsed whilst he was digging graves. Esther was also buried in the rubble but survived to become Kingston's next sextoness. The accident caused injuries which, it is said, prevented her from wearing 'stays' and as a consequence, and because of the nature of her occupation, she always afterwards wore men's clothing.

147.   (*opposite above*) Queen Victoria's Diamond Jubilee decorations in Clarence Street in 1897. The day of Queen Victoria's Jubilee, Tuesday 22 June, was heralded by a midnight peal of bells from All Saints' church which continued at intervals throughout the day. The *Surrey Comet* particularly commended Messrs. Weeks and Venn's decorations (seen in the photograph). Games were held on the Fairfield and there was a celebratory pageant on the river. The chief attraction was in the Market Place where the Borough Electrical Engineer had illuminated the Town Hall with 600 multi-coloured lamps, the letters VR standing out boldly on the towers.

148.   (*opposite below*) Silver Jubilee procession to Beverley Park on 6 May 1935. The Silver Jubilee of King George V and Queen Mary was celebrated in New Malden by 10,000 people at Beverley Park. The central attraction was an 18th-century cricket match between a team of councillors and the New Malden Cricket Club, and 3,000 children were entertained to tea in a marquee. The Women's League of Health and Beauty gave a display and the King's Speech was broadcast by loudspeaker.

150. Robert Banks Jenkinson, 2nd Earl of Liverpool (1770-1828). Lord Liverpool, Prime Minister of England from 1812 to 1827, held the position of High Steward of Kingston from 1816 until his death. Although the position was largely an honorary one, Lord Liverpool, who lived at Coombe House on Kingston Hill, took a great interest in local affairs. In 1821 he founded a charity – known as Lord Liverpool's Bounty – by which five Kingston families who had 'conducted themselves in the most orderly and proper manner during the year preceding' received £5 each at Christmas. In 1825 he laid the foundation stone for the new Kingston Bridge. Lord Liverpool was married twice, firstly on 25 March 1795 to Lady Louisa Theodosia, third daughter of Frederick Augustus Hervey, 4th Earl of Bristol, and secondly in 1822 to Miss Mary Chester, daughter of Charles Chester, and niece of the first Lord Bagot. Lord Liverpool died at Coombe House in 1828 and his funeral, handled by Hide's in the Market Place, was conducted with much pomp and circumstance. He was buried in a family vault in Hawkesbury, Gloucestershire. He was survived for 18 years by his second wife who died at Norbiton Hall. A white marble memorial to Louisa Theodosia by Chantrey stands in All Saints' church.

151. Alderman Frederick Gould, J.P. (1817-1900). Frederick Gould was born in Bath on 11 May 1817 and came to Kingston in 1839. Soon after his arrival he founded the Kingston Literary and Scientific Institution and was elected its first president. A keen collector of geological and antiquarian objects, he later donated them to the Corporation. He recalled that when he first came to the district, Surbiton was wholly agricultural or park land. There were only five buildings – a windmill and four inhabited houses – on the whole of Surbiton Hill and after the erection of the railway station the first buildings to be put up were third-class shops which ran down the left-hand side of Claremont Road (from the railway station). They had a short life, however, and were pulled down to make way for villa residences. Alderman Gould was Mayor of Kingston in 1853 and again in 1880, and interested himself in many local projects including the inauguration of the Coronation Stone in 1850 and the construction of Queen's Promenade and Canbury Gardens. He died on 23 July 1900.

152. Frederick Somner Merryweather, J.P., chairman of New Malden Local Board and Urban District Council (1827-1900). Mr. Merryweather first came to New Malden around 1860 when the population was only 900. There were no lamps, the roads were in poor condition, and the place was generally so damp and ill-cared for that he was often asked, so the story goes, whether the inhabitants of New Malden had webbed feet. He played a large part in the establishment of the New Malden Local Board and later the Urban District Council, of which he was Chairman from 1867 to 1875, and again from 1888 until his death. He did much to encourage improvements of all kinds and was instrumental in the establishment of the sewage works in 1888 and the erection of Christ Church and the National Schools. He was a member of the Kingston Board of Guardians, New Malden's representative on the County Council (from 1889) and a County Magistrate (from 1895). As editor of the *Surrey Comet*, *c.*1877-88, he wrote chatty articles under the pseudonym 'Dry as dust' and published a book *Half a Century of Kingston History* in 1887. He died aged 72 on 3 January 1900.

153. Eadweard Muybridge, pioneer of photography (1830-1904). Muybridge, pictured here in around 1894, was born and died in Kingston. He won international fame as a photographer of movement and pioneer of cinematography. He was 20 years of age when the Coronation Stone was inaugurated in 1850, and the spelling 'Eadweard' on the Stone may have influenced his adoption, later in life, of this spelling of his own name. Most of his work was undertaken in America where he survived a severe injury in a stage coach crash (1860) and a trial for the murder of his wife's lover for which he was acquitted (1875). His main claim to fame was in the successful analysis of movement by means of photography and in the development of his 'zoopraxiscope', a magic lantern projector, which enabled sequences to be seen as a moving image. He returned to Kingston in 1894 and died in 1904.

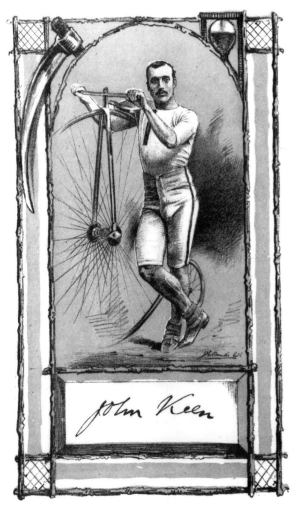

154. George William Ayliffe, hairdresser, photographer and local historian (1825-1915). George Ayliffe was born at Hampton Wick in 1825. He attended school in Hampton Wick and Surbiton – at John Boykett's establishment. Apprenticed to a hairdresser in the Apple Market in Kingston, he later had his own shops in the Apple Market, Church Street and Thames Street. He first took up photography as a hobby and in 1860 gave up hairdressing to become a photographer. He started in Kingston but moved to London for a time where he worked on an evening paper called the *Glow Worm* and met Charles Dickens. He came to Brighton Road, Surbiton, in 1870 where he remained until his retirement in 1885. From the age of seven he kept a diary recording events and changes in the area and, when he was 80, agreed to give a series of interviews to the *Surrey Comet*. These, remarkable for their accuracy, were printed in 1914 under the title *Old Kingston* in aid of the Kingston Victoria Hospital. George Ayliffe died aged 90 in 1915, at his home Glen Lyn in Richmond Road, Kingston.

155. John 'Happy Jack' Keen, famous cyclist and bicycle manufacturer (1849-1902). John Keen was born at Broadway, Worcestershire, on 25 February 1849 but he attended St Mark's School, Surbiton. He was subsequently apprenticed to a carpenter but his interest was cycling. His racing career began in 1869 when he won a race in Richmond and he soon set up business at Clapham Junction manufacturing his famous bicycle, the 'Eclipse'. He subsequently returned to Surbiton where he opened a business in Victoria Road. Later he had a workshop in a building adjoining the *Angel* public house in Thames Ditton. He gained many racing triumphs and held the mile championship until beaten by Fred Cooper in 1874 in Sheffield. He unfortunately fell upon hard times in later life and died at Finchley in January 1902.

156. Robert Cedric Sherriff (1896-1975), playwright. R. C. Sherriff was the son of
Herbert Hankin Sherriff of Aylesbury, Buckinghamshire, and Constance, daughter of
Charles Winder of Iver, Bucks. He was educated at Kingston Grammar School and
New College, Oxford. He entered the Sun Insurance Office in 1914. In 1917 he became
a Captain in the East Surrey Regiment and fought in the First World War. His first play
was written for performance in 1921 in aid of a restoration fund for Kingston Grammar
School's Lovekyn Chapel, and his most famous, *Journey's End*, based on his experiences
in the war, was performed for the first time at the Savoy Theatre in 1929. His
recreational interests included archaeology, farming and rowing, and he took a keen
interest in Kingston schools' sporting events to the end of his life. He died at Rosebriars,
Esher, in 1975.

157.   Sir Thomas Octave Murdoch (Tommy) Sopwith (1888-1989) and Harry George Hawker (1889-1921), aviation pioneers, standing next to a Sopwith 'Tabloid' twin-seat aircraft.

Thomas Sopwith (left) was born in London. In 1910 he bought an aircraft, taught himself to fly and qualified for one of the world's first aviation certificates at Brooklands. On his first solo flight in a Howard T. Wright monoplane (the first he ever owned, costing £630), he crashed after 300 yards. The aircraft was repaired and flew again soon afterwards. He went to America, won many prizes in flying competitions and returned to England to found the Sopwith Aviation Company at Kingston in 1912. One of the first aircraft he produced at the factory in Canbury Park was the Sopwith Wright Tractor which was sold to the Admiralty for £900. During the First World War he designed 31 different kinds of aircraft including the Pup, Camel, Snipe, Dolphin and Cuckoo. Tommy Sopwith, who was knighted in 1953, also took a keen interest in yachting, motorboat racing, ballooning and motor-car racing. He retired to Hampshire at the age of 75, and died aged 101 in February 1989.

Harry Hawker was born in Moorabbin in Australia in January 1889. He met Sopwith and asked him for a job to earn £50 to return to Australia but, bitten by the aeroplane 'bug', he used the money instead to pay Sopwith to teach him to fly. He joined the Sopwith Aviation Company in 1912. In the early days of the Kingston factory the aircraft were designed on the shop floor and generally took about six weeks to complete. Most of the company participated in their construction, notably Harry Hawker who also helped flight test many of the aircraft. He became Sopwith's chief test pilot during the First World War. Subsequently he won many aviation records and made an unsuccessful attempt at crossing the Atlantic in 1919 using a Sopwith Atlantic Aircraft. For this he and his fellow crewmen were awarded the Air Force Cross and were presented with £5,000 by Lord Northcliffe. He also received a rapturous homecoming from the people of Hook where he and his wife Muriel had set up home in 1917. In 1920 the Sopwith Aviation Company was wound up. A new, more diversified company was established in its place and, in recognition of Hawker's achievements, was named the H. G. Hawker Engineering Company Ltd. A more recent name for the company, Hawker Siddeley Aviation Ltd., continued the association with his name. In 1921, when he was only 32, Harry Hawker was killed at the controls of his plane during preparations for the Hendon Aerial Derby. He was buried in the churchyard of St Paul's, Hook, on 18 July 1921.

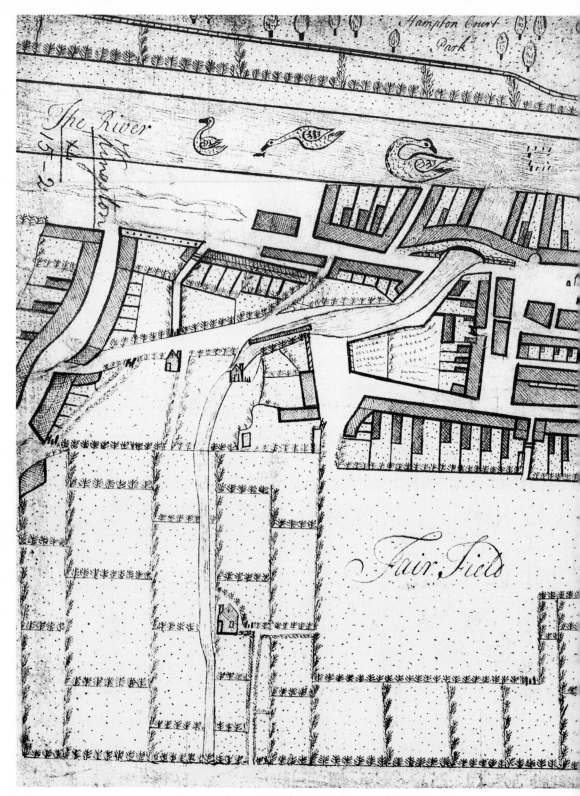

Copy of a 17th-century 'bird's eye view' of Kingston, date of copy unknown.